THE BREAD
OF THE SOUL

Third Course
Of Spiritual Maxims
Presented in Gospel's Explanations

FATHER LOUIS GUANELLA

1884

Published by
THE PIOUS UNION OF ST. JOSEPH
971 East Michigan Avenue
Grass Lake, MI 49240-9210

TRANSLATOR/EDITOR's FOREWORD

* * *

My sincere thanks to Mrs. Louise Hunter, Ed.D., Mr. & Mrs. James Rice, and Kim Bausch for their help in polishing up this translation.

The Italian texts used for this translation were those available in the Volume I of the Opera Omnia of Father Louis Guanella, published by the Centro Studi Guanelliani, Nuove Frontiere Editrice, 1992, Rome, Italy.

For the scriptural quotations, the text of the New American Bible was used.

Father Peter Di Tullio, S.C., Ed.D.
Translator/Editor

East Providence, Rhode Island, USA
Easter 1999

TABLE OF CONTENTS

* * *
*

Writings of Blessed Louis Guanella available in English

Blessed Louis Guanella
Modern Apostle of Charity

Father Guanella is an Italian priest who was beatified in 1964 and whose work of charity is a marvelous inspiration for our day.

His full name was Louis (Luigi) Guanella. He was declared Blessed by Pope Paul VI because he practiced the Christian virtues to a heroic degree, especially unbounded trust in God and a selfless love of others. He founded two religious communities, the Daughters of St. Mary of Providence and the Servants of Charity, because he wanted his work of caring for the handicapped, the sick and the aged, and of teaching the faith to go on into future generations, and he wrote many books and pamphlets because he saw millions weakening in their loyalty to Christ through ignorance of how to live their Catholic faith.

On all three levels, Father Guanella is worth knowing better. He has much to tell us Americans, whom he visited not long before he died. It was St. Pius X who encouraged the visit to America and gave Father Guanella a long autographed letter of recommendation that opened countless doors to him during his two months' travel in the United States.

Father Guanella is a model of holiness. Sanctity certainly comes from God and no one can make himself holy. But sanctity requires human cooperation, from other people and from ourselves. Both kinds of cooperation were not wanting in the life of Blessed Louis Guanella.

It all began in the home where he was born in 1842, in the mountain village of Fraciscio, north Italy, just south of Switzerland. His parents, Lawrence and Maria, had thirteen children, of whom Louis was the ninth. They were not rich but hard-working and deeply religious.

Ordained a priest in 1866, Father Guanella's next great religious influence was the privilege of having saints enter his life. First there was St. John Bosco, the founder of the Salesians, and then St. Joseph Cottolengo who organized an apostolate for the care of the poor and the sick. Later on, Father Guanella was to say, "the Lord saw to it that I should meet Don Bosco and Don Cottolengo, whom I admired and grew to love, the more I learned of them."

But there was one more saint whose role in Father Guanella's sanctity was immense. That was St. Pius X. From 1903, when he had his first private audience with the Pope, to the day Pius X died in 1914, Father Guanella received many favors from the saintly Pontiff and much financial help for his growing apostolate. But he mainly imbibed from St. Pius X the twin spirit of firmness in the Catholic faith and total reliance on Divine Providence in doing the will of God.

Not surprisingly, Father Guanella's growth in holiness was provided not only by friendly people but by enemies. Opposition stalked his path almost as soon as he began his works of charity, and he was not without foes to the day of his death. This is so true that one could almost write a biography of Blessed Louis Guanella, built on the episodes of criticism and even open persecution he experienced over the years both from state and Church authorities. Yet he never rebelled against authority, no matter how painfully it was sometimes exercised. Actually, opposition only served to strengthen his dependence on God and assurance that his work must be pleasing to the Lord, seeing how angry it made the enemies of Christ and His Church.

Father Guanella's charity was distinctive, because of the helplessness of those he sought to reach. When asked by the civil authorities what he planned to do, he answered without hesitation, "I want to gather the orphans, the aged, the deaf, the blind, the mentally deficient, the crippled, the epileptics, the invalids, and all who are in danger of being treated as the castoffs of society." That is what he did, and that is what his followers, the Daughters of St. Mary of Providence and the Servants of Charity were charged with.

The final dimension of Blessed Louis Guanella is, perhaps, the least well known. His monumental achievements of the social apostolate have obscured what he did as a teacher of the faith.

It must be pointed out that Father Guanella was not a speculator. He was a man of action even in his writings, which are extensive, over fifty books and pamphlets. He wrote about every conceivable aspect of the faith; but he was not a theorist. He was practical. His concern in writing was not so much to explain what is the faith, as to tell people how to live the faith. His main interest in publishing was not to analyze Catholic belief, but help Catholics apply what they believe to their daily lives -- in every state of life and not only priests and religious.

As we look more closely at his writings, we find they focus on these directives, "Pray!" "Love!" and "Suffer!" Taught by someone else, they might be three catch words. But they are burning with meaning in Father Louis Guanella.

Father Guanella's work and teaching are an answer that every true follower of Christ, in every walk of life, needs to hear and see: that we love God only if we love our neighbor.

Who is Father Guanella? He is a person very much alive in his communities and writings today. He is a person who took the Gospels literally and whose message of honesty in charity has never been more timely than today.

(From Fr. John Hardon, S.J.:
Father Guanella - Modern Apostle of Charity)

With this booklet, published by the Eusebiana Printing Co. in Milan, in 1884 (cm 13x10, pp. 362) and set as part of the series, Il Cattolico Provveduto (The Well-equipped Catholic), *Father Guanella completed the publication of his triple course of homilies on Sunday Gospels.*

The front cover carries the indication of Vol. 3, *while the title-page carries the motto,* Viva sempre il SS. Sacramento (Long live the Most Blessed Sacrament). *The last page of the text is concluded with the permit for publication,* Admittitur / Joseph Bossi Parochus / Censor Ecclesiasticus, *with no indication of place and date.*

The homily for the third Sunday after Epiphany carries an internal chronological reference to 1883, that might indicate this year as the period of time during which this book was written.

Both in content and argumentation this text depends on the collection of daily meditations, The manna of the soul, *written by the Jesuit Father Paul Segneri (1624-1694). Each excerpt taken from Segneri as a source can be easily recognized by the scriptural reference which Segneri put "in esergo", while Father Guanella inserts it in the homily.*

The second edition of this booklet was published in 1929 under the editing care of Father Leonardo Mazzucchi, as part of the series, Bibliotechina di operette ascetico-morali di Don Luigi Guanella (The Little Library of Ascetical-moral Writings of Father Louis Guanella), *# 22-23 under the title,* Il pane dell'anima - Terzo corso di massime scritturali esposte nelle spiegazioni evangeliche di ogni domenica da Don Luigi Guanella (The bread of the soul -

Third course of scriptural maxims presented in the explanation of the Gospels of every Sunday by Father Louis Guanella), *Como - House of Divine Providence, 1929, pp. 382. The editing work was limited to a brief preface and a few interventions in cleaning up the text from typographical errors as well as to render it more clear in a few passages.*

THE BREAD OF THE SOUL

Third Course
Of Spiritual Maxims
Presented in Gospel's Explanations

GOSPEL OF THE FIRST SUNDAY
OF ADVENT

The winnowing-fan in the hands of the judge

1. People live a very troubled life here on earth. In a special way there are Christians who suffer even though they are good. They are afflicted by brothers and sisters who persecute them openly or covertly. How sad it is to see innocent people persecuted! Yet, keep up your courage, my brothers and sisters. A day will come when a separation will be made. Then good people will receive their reward, while the evil ones will receive the punishment they deserve. There is no doubt. The Lord has given his word on this. Behold what St. Luke the evangelist writes in this regard.

Jesus said to his disciples: "There will be signs in the sun, the moon and the stars. On the earth, nations will be in anguish, distraught at the roaring of the sea and the waves. Men will die of fright in anticipation of what is coming upon the earth. The powers in the heavens will be shaken. After that, men will see the Son of Man coming on a cloud with great power and glory".[1]

My brothers and sisters, let us take a look at the majesty of Jesus Christ who comes to us. He comes to do justice on earth. He wants good people to be recognized and the evil one to be condemned. The same St. Luke presents Jesus like a farmer rather than a city dweller. He is carrying his winnowing-fan in his right hand and makes everyone know that he is going to clear the threshing floor of his

---

[1] Lk 21: 25-27

Church. Following are the textual words: "His winnowing-fan is in his hand. He will clear the threshing floor and gather his grain into his granary; but the chaff he will burn in unquenchable fire."[1]

Divine Savior, Oh how just will all people find you on that day! Still we now adore you with reverence within this temple. And we desire to appear before you with reverence and love on the day when you will judge the world.

2. Here on earth the Church of Jesus includes good people as well as evil individuals. At times one who is good is portrayed as evil, while an evil individual is treated as an honest and pious one. The Church of Christ here on earth is like a threshing floor where good grain is mingled with the chaff.

Does the farmer have to work hard to clear his wheat? Not at all, for actually this operation of separating the wheat from the chaff takes a minute. He holds his winnowing-fan, which is just a wooden shovel, throws the wheat into the air just a little and sees to it that the good wheat falls on one place while the chaff piles up far from it. Likewise our judge, Jesus Christ, in a moment will separate the good from the evil. We will see it then! The hypocrites who have tried to deceive such a large number of people on earth, will be uncovered. The feigned idle people as well as all those who secretly chafed with anger or jealousy or any other even more evil passion, will all be unmasked on that day in all their lives. The evil ones will be very greatly grieved and embarrassed. On the contrary it will be necessary that at last the good people will be justified in the presence of all the world.

---

[1] Lk 3:17

3. Jesus Christ is the supreme judge. He is the eternal wisdom who scrutinizes everything, who holds everything present in his sight. He is infinite wisdom. Don't think at all that even a single thought of one's mind or the littlest affection of one's heart may be hidden from him!

Jesus Christ is the supreme judge, because as the Father, by his grace, lifts souls from the state of sin to the state of grace, so Jesus Christ raises the bodies from the state of death to the state of life. Then all the dead will rise to stand before Jesus who will judge them. It is right that one who has to be judged see his own judge. Yet the reprobates would not be able to see him unless Jesus came in person as the Man God.

After all, wasn't Jesus Christ condemned as guilty by the lowest and most iniquitous tribunals? Do you remember how Jesus in the presence of Caiaphas received a sharp blow on the face, and how he was mocked in the presence of Pilate? Isn't it right now that Jesus comes in person to men and makes himself recognized in all the glory of his majesty?... Then, how can one, who finds out that he has abused Jesus with vile blasphemies, and is told that more than once he has profaned the blood of the Savior, be able to stand there and watch? Yet the evil wretched ones will be forced to stand there until Jesus has pointed them out to everyone and has condemned them.

4. Behold all men gathered for the universal judgment. They are innumerable, since there are all the descendants of Adam for eight thousand years to our very days. There will also be all the people who will be born after us until the end of the world.

These people, endless in number, as I said, will be mingled by faith and customs. There will be Hebrews along with Moslems, Moslems along with faithful Christians. What will take place, then? There is no doubt.

The Hebrews who heard Jesus Christ preach and afterwards did not follow him, will be condemned all together in a bundle. The unfaithful people who saw Jesus Christ climb Calvary, yet cursed him horribly, will also be condemned but in a lesser way, according to justice and without delay, as it is done to rebels in time of war. Christians will be there. These people, who cost Jesus Christ his most holy blood, and whom Jesus loved so much through his most sacred Sacraments, will also be screened with the winnowing-fan. My God, will plenty of chaff for burning be found among Christians? Horrible sight! Chaff and straw are very flammable in a whirlwind of fire once started!

5. Then, all will know how just the Lord is, and will find out why the Lord left them here on earth mingled together, the good ones with the evil ones. The wheat is supported and nourished by the straw and the chaff, even though God could have the grain result by itself out of the soil. Admirable is the wisdom of God who knows how to obtain good even out of evil itself.

In every home there are individuals who are troublesome and evil. In every town there are very wicked persecutors, as every era has its own war even within the Church of our divine Savior. At the final judgment we will come to know how the evil ones gave a happy chance to the good people to exercise patience, humility, and detachment from earthly things. The good people will appear like the wheat that for each grain produces a hundredfold. How happy will they be in finding themselves to be treated like the chosen wheat! Their joy will be equal in amount to the calamity which the reprobates will experience at seeing themselves to be like the lifeless chaff, annoying and abominable!

6. All along, the good ones will gather around God. Here on earth they were scattered everywhere to the east and to the west, to the north as well as to the south, to lands where barbarians live, in order to give greater glory to the Lord and to convert them. Once that final day of judgment will come, all the good people will be assembled in holy rejoicing around the Lord. The souls in purgatory will be freed from there and added here to this chosen gathering. At seeing one another, they will all break into a song of joy, and hymns of thanksgiving and praise. They will see that they are with God, rejoicing greatly for being blessed.

7. On the contrary, the reprobates will be driven back below to burn like a pile of straw in flames of fire. How quick and powerfully does straw burn in a fiery furnace! Likewise will the souls of the wicked burn in hell. Don't even think whether they will ever stop suffering! It is written that the chaff will burn in an unquenchable fire. That fire is set by the justice of God, ready to vindicate every grave sin. The divine anger will enkindle it like the wind in a hurricane. The unfortunate who will burn there will feel the burden of being useless straw and shameful chaff, while they had a chance to be chosen wheat!

Finally the judgment is over, and the verdict is given. The souls of the just will rise to the granary of the heavenly Father, in paradise. The souls of the wicked will fall down into the depths, where like chaff they will be burned without ever being consumed. What will happen to each of us on that day?... We will be what we persevere in being in the present time. We will be good wheat if we produce excellent fruits of good deeds. Yet if one of us is now straw of indifference and chaff of scandal and ruin, if he perseveres in his foolishness, will no doubt be straw and chaff good for the unquenchable fire in hell.

REFLECTIONS

1. The winnowing-fan in the hands of the judge.
2. The Church of Jesus Christ is a threshing floor that will be purged at the end of the world.
3. Jesus Christ will come to judge the just and the unjust.
4. All men will be gathered.
5. Then everyone will know why God let the good people live here on earth mingled with the wicked ones.
6. The just will gather to praise God.
7. The wicked ones will be driven down to burn in hell.

GOSPEL OF THE SECOND SUNDAY OF ADVENT

Keep your eyes open on your way

1. The Hebrews were very tired of waiting for the coming of the heavenly guide who was going to lead them to paradise. Then they saw a man named Jesus, living in the desert like an angel, and acting in the city like one who was able to work miracles, healing the sick, raising the dead, and preaching a doctrine from heaven. Many people crowded around John, who, in learning about that miracle worker, sent a deputation to Jesus to ask him: "Are you the Messiah, the savior, or do we look for someone else?" Jesus was surrounded by a crowd of listeners whom he was teaching. He kept healing the sick and working more miracles, then, answering their question he said: "You have seen: report to John what you have learned." The messengers left. The divine Savior spoke to the crowds and said: "When you went to the desert to hear John, what did you find? A reed swaying in the wind? Or someone luxuriously dressed? In seeing John you found a prophet indeed and something more: an angel who prepares the way to the Lord."[1]

Brothers and sisters, we are all on our way to paradise. On the way there, let us pay attention to the road we are walking on. Along the way there are dangers we must avoid, and directions we must follow. The kingly Psalmist said: "My eyes are ever toward the Lord, for he will free my feet from

---

[1] See Mt 11: 2-10

the snare."[1] We are on the road, who will save us from dangers? Let us keep our eyes open on our journey. Let us look up to the one who saves us.

2. We find ourselves on a road that is long, dangerous, intricate. There is the danger of falling at every step we take. There are dangers that come from wild beasts and men who may assault us. Where are we going to keep our eyes? Not on our feet, for this is not enough. We have to look on high. If we call on God for help, he will care for us. If he takes care of us, we will be saved for certain. Safe will be the child who cries out for his father's help, safe will the servant be who turns pitifully to his master for help.

3. Here, think about all the attentions a servant displays toward his master. St. Pauline, bishop of Nola, not knowing what else to do to free the Christians who had been taken into slavery, turned himself in as a slave to free the son of a widow. As a slave, he made use of his attention to find out what his master liked most. Early in the morning he would arrange a fragrant bouquet of flowers and would bring it to his master with affection, so that he would enjoy it first thing in the morning. One day the prince asked him: "Who are you?..." St. Pauline answered: "I am a bishop from Italy." "Well, then," the prince said, "I free you from these labors, from these dangers. Feel free to return to Italy and to your diocese."

To incline the Lord to have mercy for us, we have to keep our eyes toward him always, and find out what he likes most to receive from us. Let us study the inclinations of the heart of Jesus, let us ponder on the most holy attributes of the

---

[1] Ps 25(24): 15

Most High, and let us grow thoughts in our minds that we know will please him. With our hands let us carry out deeds that we know will please him greatly.

4. Furthermore we must keep up with the example given to us by Jesus Christ. What an honor to be able to accompany the king of paradise! We can accompany him to the cave in Bethlehem and on his way to Egypt. We can be with him in the shop in Nazareth, and then on the field of his preaching in Judea and Galilee. All of us can accompany him to Jerusalem and to Calvary.

Two conditions are called for to meet this end. First of all we have to think with our mind and ask ourselves: what would Jesus do in this very moment when I am speaking and acting? Then, we have to pay attention to fulfill diligently all the tasks which God expects of us.

5. While doing this, let us pray to God and he will hear us. What does a servant need from his master? In a special way he needs to ask him for pardon for all his failures. He needs to ask him to give him help in his life needs and protect him from dangers. Finally, the servant needs to show to his excellent master all those signs of gratitude possible to him.

We are expected to do likewise. We should accompany Jesus Christ and in the meantime we should ask for his pardon, his help, his assistance against dangers. Isn't this helpful? Then, saying words of affection and thanksgiving wouldn't it be a dear task for us? Let us keep doing so and we will be faithful servants of our Lord.

6. The good Lord will snatch us from all dangers. A danger for us is the possibility of missing the way, yet if we obey the Lord, he will even send an angel to us, if necessary,

as he sent one to St. Bernard whenever he needed it. Thus we will journey safely. We need strength in our journey and we can obtain it following the example of Jesus who leads us. Who can look at the divine Savior who starts out as a giant and then slows down the pace on the way of good? Hastening on our way, we need to be delivered from all the snares of our adversary. We obtain this through prayer. A child or a servant who cries out for help, is immediately heard by his father or his master. How much quicker is the Lord in saving us from the many dangers that surround us!

Look at St. Aloysius Gonzaga. He was living in the midst of a debauchering court, of blaspheming soldiers, surrounded by companions and relatives who employed all means to dissuade him from serving God with perfection. Aloysius found himself at times ensnared by the furor of fire, at other times by raging waters. Nontheless, he was able to overcome his relatives, to laugh at his companions, to tread upon the softnesses of life and obtain what he wanted most at all cost, to be able to enter the way to perfection and his own sanctification in religious life.

Likewise we must sanctify ourselves. The means is simple, as I have told you so far. It is enough that in journeying we keep our eyes open, looking toward our Lord.

REFLECTIONS

1. Keep your eyes open on your way.
2. We are on the path that leads us from the earth to heaven.
3. Let us discover what work or journey God desires us to take or do.
4. All along let us act with uprightness, as Jesus Christ gives us the example.

5. In journeying, let us ask from God whatever we need.
6. The Lord will answer us and will save us from all dangers.

GOSPEL OF THE THIRD SUNDAY OF ADVENT

Look at your iniquities

1. This morning the saddest image of penance comes to us, John the Baptist. His chest is wide open, his face is fiery because of the ardor of his emotions. He is clothed in lamb's skin, barefoot, wearing no hat. He hastens in the wilderness crying out, urging everyone who approaches him for advice to do penance. He urges everyone: "Do penance!"

Today, then, noble messengers picked from among the leaders of the people came to question him: "Who are you, so that we may honor you as you deserve? Are you a prophet, or Elijah come back to life, or are you the Savior himself?" John answered: "No, I am not the Messiah, nor Elijah, nor a prophet. I am a voice in the desert, crying out: Do penance! I baptize you with water of penance. There is the Savior among you, the strap of whose sandals I am not worthy to unfasten."[1] Afterwards he dismissed the importunate questioning of the messengers and turned to address the crowds, urging everyone: "Do penance!"

Let us do penance ourselves! The Lord is going to show himself to us, also. How will we be able to meet him, we sinners, unless we at least offer him a contrite heart? The holy king, David, though aware that his sin had been forgiven already by God, nonetheless he kept repeating to the Lord: "Thoroughly wash me from my guilt and of my sin cleanse me. For I acknowledge my offense, and my sin is before me

---

[1] See Jn 1: 19-28

always."[1] We, too, are wretched sinners. Let us learn how to be sorry for our sins, as the Gospel and the kingly Psalmist suggest to us.

2. In the Sacred Scripture we read how a child went with his mother to the field and there was struck with a terrible headache. He cried out to his mother: "My head hurts, my head hurts!" In such a compassionate state he kept crying out until he died.

Oh, what a headache mortal sin is!... Mortal sin is not just a headache, but it is a pain in the heart, a torment for the entire body and for all the faculties of the soul as well. In the garden of Gethsemane, because of mortal sins, our divine Savior was in agony, sweating blood from his face and his entire body. Peter, the apostle, wept all his life because of his triple mortal sin. He wept so much that two grooves carved his face eversince. The Lord had forgiven Peter for his enormous sin, yet the tender heart of the apostle, reflecting upon the majesty and goodness of God offended by him on one hand and the iniquity of his sin on the other, seemed to be able to find comfort nowhere else other than in crying every day more heartily.

Likewise we should have our eyes wet with tears until the end. He who weeps will obtain a more hearty forgiveness and greater graces. We need to weep until the end, for crying is the best thing wretched sinners can do.

3. We do not regret our sins with an abundance of tears because we do not deeply know their malice. Let us think of a young man who, from being the first son of a king, has become the slave of a very barbarian tyrant. He wails in a

---

[1] Ps 51(50): 4-5

dark dungeon, afflicted by the torment of leprosy and pestilence. After losing everything, he is waiting at any time to see the door of the dungeon open to be taken to his final capital punishment. Poor young man! What a pity for such a wretched young man!

If we have sinned, let us turn to weeping in regret for our faults. A soul that has fallen from the state of grace into the snare of sin is a child of the Lord who, after leaving the heavenly palace, goes down into the dungeon of hell. Mortal sin is a hell for souls. As a consequence, how much such a wretched individual should be sorry! Let us all be sorry, because mortal sin is the worst evil that can fall upon a Christian soul.

4. Let us consider the iniquity of a Christian more closely. King Nabuchednezzar had a golden statue representing himself built. He had all the people assembled and told them: "Adore me as a god before that statue, since I am a god equal to the Most High. Adore me, or you all will die." Antiochus, a very cruel king, waited for all the people to be gathered in a certain place and then he had all of them slaughtered like sheep. King Saul, waging war on his enemies and losing the battle, leaned on his spear to kill himself miserably.

Most detestable excesses! Yet, when a Christian individual wide awake and cold bloodedly commits a sin of such malice, is like a wretched individual who kills himself with a knife, and oftentimes kills the soul of his neighbor with the spear of scandal. With a javelin of impiety he throws aloft, he aims at waging war on the Most High. Then, you tell me how an individual with mortal sin in his soul does not become a detestable monstrosity!

5. More so, if we ponder on the fact that sin always leaves behind its most dismal consequences. First among these is the inclination of a sinful habit. It may very well happen that an individual does not die of an illness or wound or articulation of the joints, yet that illness leaves a special flaw in one's body that makes it prone to many other diseases. For this reason, they must all be certainly avoided.

The wound of a mortal sin leaves in one's soul a lack of strength, a propensity to relapse, which can cause serious troubles to a Christian if he does not keep himself consistently alert to it. Hence the need for weeping over our sins, so that the remnants of our iniquities can be cured to the very last scar left on our soul. Hence the need for us to weep continually so that we may not fall into any sin again.

St. Catherine, after seeing in a vision the horror of sin, wept in desolation. St. Magdalene De' Pazzi begged God to lay across the gate of hell in order to prevent all souls from falling into it. We all pray that everyone may be saved. Let us pray for ourselves so that we may put our souls in safety.

6. Therefore, working a miracle of mercy for the sake of a sinner, God is asked to have pity on the wretched one. All along we are expected to cry out to the Most High. Then God expects of us the sacrifice of repentance and many good deeds.

At this point he adds to it the impulse of his grace and the benefit of his mercy. The branch produces its grapes as long as it is attached to the vine from which it receives vigor. A Christian draws his life from the grace that is the strength of Jesus Christ. Out of his ineffable mercy, our divine Savior has given the Sacrament of Penance, by which a sinner is justified because of the fruit of Jesus' blood. The blood of

Jesus Christ heals human frailties and clothes the soul with heavenly virtues.

7. St. Aloysius Gonzaga wept over two minor faults of his life with tears that poured out of his eyes his entire life. Because of one very serious sin, King David clothed his body with hair-shirts, wore ashes on his head, and never stopped weeping. Doing so, they learned more and more to detach themselves from the demands of the flesh. At the same time they inflicted more lashes of defeat to the devil. This is the result of a consistent weeping.

How much do we detest our sins? If we do not detest them to the high degree we have indicated, it is a sign that we have not yet renounced the follies of the world, the deceits of Satan, and the iniquitous demands of concupiscence.

REFLECTIONS

1. One forever regrets a very wicked evil.
2. A mortal sin hurts one's soul more vividly than a torment in his body.
3. A grave sin is a cruel misfortune.
4. It is a frightful monstrosity that in one shot carries out three murders.
5. Even after being forgiven, mortal sin leaves behind an inclination to evil in one's soul.
6. Weeping and doing good deeds are the only comforts left for a sinner.
7. Thus a Christian renounces the follies of sin and sets himself to become a saint.

GOSPEL OF THE FOURTH SUNDAY OF ADVENT

A virgin soil sprouts the Just One

1. As soon as you find out that you are walking on hot grounds, you realize that you are in the midst of a cursed land. How welcomed is the restoring rain over those burning rocks!

The soil of this world was burning under the feet of its inhabitants because of so many iniquities. Men could not stand it any longer. Uniting themselves in spirit with the holy prophets who were able to foresee the future, cried out with longing: "Let justice descend, O heavens, like dew from above, like gentle rain let the skies drop it down. Let the earth open and salvation bud forth."[1]

The prophet, John Baptist, seeing the Savior coming soon, kept preaching the baptism of penance for the remission of sins. He preached along with it what is written in the book in the words of Isaiah the prophet: "A herald's voice in the desert, crying, 'Make ready the way of the Lord, clear him a straight path. Every valley shall be filled and every mountain and hill shall be leveled. The windings shall be made straight and the rough ways smooth, and all mankind shall see the salvation of God."[2]

We, too, see the longing of humankind. Let us raise our eyes above and with blissful exultation let us exclaim:

---

[1] Is 45:8
[2] Lk 3: 1-6

"We thank you, O Lord, that from the virgin soil of Mary buds forth the Savior."

2. When the Lord appeared again on the earth and found it for the first time stained with the horrible sin of rebellion, he said to it: "You shall not give any fruit to man unless he labors from the sweat of his brow!" From then on the earth was stained with numberless wickednesses, thereby becoming like the ground of an infernal volcano.

Men were waiting to discover a virgin land capable of restoring the wickedness of the earth, yet how long was it taking to find it! Though late, it was found at last and it appeared so much more beautiful indeed. A blessed soil was the virgin heart of Mary. What an innocent era! What a fruitful soil, what a virginal enclosure! Going through her the Just One par excellence, that is the Savior, not only her virginity was not darkened, on the contrary she was beautified like a crystal that becomes more splendid when the rays of the sun go through it.

What a purity! Remember that when the archangel said: "You will become the mother of the Savior," she was troubled and did not seem to be reassured until the same angelic spirit said to her: "What will happen to you will be the work of the Holy Spirit, and becoming a mother you will not cease from remaining a most pure virgin".

3. Heaven was touched by the longing of so many patriarchs of this earth, was touched by the longings of so many prophets, as well as by the cries of so many just people of this earth. God let the heavenly dew descend upon them. How did he do it? Little by little Mary proved to be fertile, even before the mystery was uncovered. Little by little in

Bethlehem and in Nazareth, in Jerusalem and all over the world, this heavenly dew descended.

In regard to place and people, this dew first of all touched the land of Palestine and the Hebrew nation, leaving the rest of the world sterile. Afterwards this dew expanded to all the world, leaving the Hebrew people sterile. Thus Gideon saw that the dew one night covered the lamb's skin laid on the threshingfloor, but the following night the dew covered the threshingfloor leaving the lamb's skin untouched. Likewise this heavenly dew descends upon the soil of Christian hearts. Little by little it bedews them with the dew of its blessings and lays then in abundance with its fruits, when the soil of our surroundings proves to be receptive to his divine graces.

4. Heavens rained down the dew, Mary gave birth to the Savior. What and how great a blessing! The appearance of a just man on earth consoles the hearts of a numerous nation. Often a just individual is an angel of salvation. In our days how much recreated we feel by the presence of an individual whom we consider sent by Divine Providence to restore the damages of society!

Yet the one born of the Virgin Mary is not an ordinary upright individual. He is the just one par excellence. He is not just because of grace granted to him: he is just per essence, by origin and his very nature. The just one we talk about is the Savior, come down from heaven out of the mercy of the Eternal Father. How heartily we should embrace this just one! A soil burnt by the sun does not welcome a fecundating rain as eagerly as the children of sin welcome the just one who comes to restore them. Come, Just One of God, come, O Savior of the world, and do not delay.

5. Coming, Jesus rescues us from the disease of sin and frees us from the punishment that we deserve. Think of an unfortunate individual who, after drinking at the chalice of lewdness, comes back covered with sores like a leper. Imagine how, once he is found out to be so, he is taken to a shameful place of punishment. How good this unfortunate individual would feel if, paying, he could find someone able to free him from the torment of that evil and from the shame of that punishment!

We are those miserable wretched ones. Not once, but many times we have soiled ourselves with sin and now more than one punishment weighs upon our backs. Yet we have to make recourse to Jesus with confidence. We will entrust ourselves to him with joy. Jesus comes to save us. Realizing that a friend has traveled a very long journey to come to see us, how heartily we would embrace him! Just so, Jesus Christ has journeyed from heaven to earth. How much comfort should his coming bring to our hearts!

Blessed Mother of the Savior, Immaculate Virgin, we entrust ourselves to you so that you may lead us to the arms of Jesus our Savior, of Jesus the Just One whom you have produced from the virgin soil of your holy womb.

REFLECTIONS

1. A virgin soil produces the Just One.
2. Mary is that virgin soil.
3. Upon her the heavenly dew descended.
4. Mary gave birth to the Just One.
5. He rescues us from the evil of sin and from the punishment we deserve.

GOSPEL OF THE SUNDAY
WITHIN THE OCTAVE
OF HOLY CHRISTMAS

A sample of Catholic doctrine

1. When the devil wants to deceive men more miserably, he appears to them under the form of a good spirit, and apparently holds salutary discourses. In the meantime, since the devil is a spirit though evil, he employs a subtle approach to seduce souls. If we take a close look, we realize that the most scandalous heresies which have ruined such a great number of Christians, crept into them with great cunning shrewdness and subtlety.

In these days a heresy has raised its monstrous head high and is saluted as a queen wherever she is welcomed as their mistress. There are towns and individuals who know how to detect this abominable one and speak loudly against it as it deserves. Yet, at the same time, they do not leave out fondling certain doctrines that flatter the senses and their own satisfactions so much.

Let us take as an example the teaching of Jesus Christ who says: do good to all... forgive your enemies... do not take any revenge against anyone... it is better to mortify oneself here on earth in order to deserve a reward in heaven. This is a sample of Catholic Christian doctrine. Yet the liberals oppose this teaching by stating: bearing with something is good when you are forced to.... forgiving and not taking revenge generally is not expedient, because everyone must care for his good reputation...

So, we have two teachers; which one should we believe?... It is better to believe Jesus Christ. You might say: is there anyone who still literally believes in the gospel's maxims? I answer to this question with today's Gospel.

"The divine Savior was only a few days old when he was taken to the temple where two elderly individuals met with him, Simeon and Anna. One of these, without dodging the point, said to Jesus' mother, 'This child is destined to be the downfall and the rise of many in Israel, a sign that will be opposed - and you yourself shall be pierced with a sword - so that the thoughts of many hearts may be laid bare.' Anna, also, gave thanks to God and talked about the child to all who looked forward to the deliverance of Jerusalem".[1]

How do you feel about this?... Jesus Christ came to teach the truth and everyone should have believed in him, yet here Simeon foresees that he will become a target at which everyone will attempt to aim. Jesus and his doctrine still remain a target today. How many oppose him!

Do these people deserve a good reputation? On the contrary, they deserve the greatest reproach. See what St. Paul wrote to Timothy about them: "Whoever teaches in any other way, not holding to the sound doctrines of our Lord Jesus Christ and the teaching proper to true religion, should be recognized as both conceited and ignorant, a sick man in his passion for polemics and controversy."[2] Miserable, indeed, is he who claims to know better than Jesus Christ. I want to give you a sample of the Catholic doctrine that regards forgiving. We will, then, see how wretched are the reasons produced by those who oppose the maxims of the gospel.

---

[1] See Lk 2: 33-40
[2] 1 Tm 6: 3-4

2. In the midst of a Christian world we find a pagan monstrosity. It is a statue made of mud, it is the image of every vice and error. It is what is called the divinity of vicious materialism and philosophical rationalism. And there are people who kneel before that image and say: "You are my god". There are other people who shun doing so, yet they look to it from afar and they fall short from taking off their hat before it. These latter ones are not individuals with no faith, no, yet how poor they are in professing the doctrine of the divine Savior!

Let us consider the case brought to our attention by St. Paul. He says that there are individuals who do not hold to the sound doctrines of our Lord Jesus Christ. Who are they? Too many to be counted. Some surpass all others, by claiming that we are not expected to forgive since that is too hard to do, that we must not forgive because it is shameful for a Christian not to be able to prove who he is and have his reasons respected. All along, they never hold both in mind and heart the teachings of our savior Jesus Christ. There are others who state this both in speech and in action categorically. Can these be called Christians? They are Christians by name but actually pagans. There are others who say so by hints, but in fact they try to obey the precept of the Lord. These people cannot be condemned but encouraged so that with more lively affection they might believe the word of Jesus who is the truth per essence.

3. Poor divine Savior! He comes on earth to tell us: "Love God who is the father of all, respect your brothers and sisters who are all children of God. Love everyone." Yet these who are reluctant to forgive, by their action demonstrate to know better than God himself. They are ambitious individuals who attempt to upset the house of the Father. Jesus says:

"Love the Lord and his children." Thus he teaches a most pious doctrine meant to bring peace and love on earth as far as even to heaven. Yet these individuals who teach that we are not supposed to forgive, actually are impious individuals who deny the word of God, they are impious individuals who ill-treat the person of their neighbor.

Imagine that someone comes into your home and incites your children to rebel against their father, and to wage war against one another in the family; how long would you tolerate that wicked revolutionary?... See, then, how can God be pleased with those individuals who directly or indirectly somehow stir hatred and do not appease contentions!

4. Yet this is the predominant vice in our century. Do you want to know why so many come around to make judgments so foolishly in regard to God and religion? The reason is that there are too many who are proud and are ignorant. When one is ignorant, he does not even want to believe others' discourses. He does not understand them, interprets them in his own way, disdains even to listen to them. As ignorant as one is, so he is proud. He scorns everyone and makes fun of everything.

Many times our ears have to listen to such discourses that horrify one who still believes in Jesus the savior. Many individuals say: "My reason is enough for everything... I will do nothing but what my intelligence tells me and man's common sense suggests". Thus they reject the judgment of the pope, they separate themselves from dealing with the priests, ridicule those scriptural maxims that, being of divine origin, should be adored as the very person of the Incarnate Word.

These people state that forgiving degrades man. Are we going to believe the word of man more than God's word? Listen and be horrified! The Lord says: "What man thinks important, God holds in contempt."[1] Let no ignorant individual be in our midst, that is one who is proud and knows nothing, yet makes judgments as if he knew better.

5. All along we are moved to pity in seeing how these individuals linger around frivolous matters wasting time with conflicting words. In regard to matters, they do not discuss anything better than the shabbiness of their honor and material goods. Is, perhaps, the smoke of honor that makes man great, or a handful of mire that makes him fortunate? Let him who has wisdom think about it!

Valiant is the mind of those illustrious people who, by the power of their talent and the constancy of their will, end up with discovering what is best admired then by the entire world in matters of industry or Christian art. St. Francis Xavier, who in the brief period of ten years traveled so much as going around the world five times, and baptized over two-hundred thousand people; St. Theresa of Avila who reformed the entire Carmelite Order and established over thirty monasteries; St. Francis DeSales who in one day converted sixty thousand enraged Calvinists: these are the ones who prove to have power of intelligence.

Yet the other ones of whom we are talking about here, place the entire life of man in the vanity of honor, in a handful of goods which soon become shameful egotism, the entire expression of their activities. Furthermore, as enervated they are in action, so frivolous they become in talking. An honorific title becomes a matter of great undertaking that takes their effort. For a title of honor they fight in dispute, for a title of honor they get into fights with one another at times even to the point of bloodshed. These are the great ones of the

---

[1] Lk 16:15

world! Let those who want to do so value that greatness; I abhor it. God's wrath and indignation is reserved for these wretched ones. I, for my part, choose to become the people's target as Jesus, my savior, was. A holy maxim of the gospel's teaching is better than the corrupted doctrine of a lying world.

REFLECTIONS

1. A sample of Catholic doctrine in the midst of liberal contradictions.
2. A statue of a pagan divinity in the midst of Christianity.
3. Jesus Christ teaches the mercy of forgiveness, yet so many people oppose him.
4. The ignorant and the proud oppose him.
5. These individuals linger around vain matters, and get lost with conflicting words.

GOSPEL OF THE FIRST SUNDAY
AFTER EPIPHANY

Glorious victory

1. The dearest day in life for a man is the one in which he has won over his implacable adversary. In the Capitol of ancient Rome there was an arch of triumph and an amphitheater to solemnize the celebrations of the heroes.

Man's implacable adversaries are his senses that wage war on reason. However, once man has overcome these adversaries, he deserves greater praises than Caesar or Hannibal or Pirrus did in the glory of their expeditions. It is easier to win over an equipped army than win over one's very self.

The divine Savior gives us a most noble example in this battle of submitting our senses to the spirit. An angel appears to Joseph and says: "Take the child and his mother and come to the land of Judah." Joseph sets himself on the way there and Jesus follows in his footsteps. Once returned to Nazareth, Jesus remains always obedient to Mary and Joseph. One day the Eternal Father told him clearly to go to the temple to speak to the teachers. He went there and stayed there for three days. When Mary and Joseph found him, Jesus quickly told them: "I obeyed in doing something for the glory of my eternal Father." He, then, immediately joined them and returned to Nazareth where he was obedient to them until he reached the age of thirty.[1]

---

[1] See Lk 2:42-52

Behold our victory: to obey in order to mortify one's appetites. The Lord says in his *Proverbs*: "He who listens will finally have his say."[1] Let us try to understand this truth and let us pray that God may enlighten us to ascertain it well so that we may learn how to practice it.

2. You see a lion in the forest. When he wants to show his power, he roars and makes the tigers of the land tremble. You see an eagle in the skies. To prove that he is the king of all the birds, he rises above all of them and by whirling ascents he rises close to the sun.

In the waters you see the whale. When he wants to stand out above all the fishes or cetaceans of the sea, he opens his mouth and swallows thousands of little fish, releases one of his fins on his back and shoots up a whistling column of water that towers high revealing the colors of the iris. If a ship comes close, the whale makes it sink by a knock of his tail or by overturning it with its back. These animals are powerful and win over others, yet do they deserve much praise? Not at all. They do nothing but carry out what their instinct tells them according to their nature.

Man is the one who really deserves in the highest degree. He is the one who can perform a work of well-being or a work of ruin, for he is free. Now if he holds to good, by restraining his passions, he is assured that by winning over himself he obtains a much greater victory. His victory is greater than the victory Moses obtained in dividing the waters of the Red Sea, greater than Joshua's in stopping the sun on its course, greater than Samson's when with his fist killed lions. Do you wonder, then, that you can become victorious and illustrious yourselves?

---

[1] Prv 21:28

31

3. I want to list for you the victories which you easily can obtain by obeying. The first victory is the one over all the evil beasts of your sinful passions. A person who is perfectly obedient is a saint. He who obeys to please God has achieved for himself a queen virtue surrounded by maids like humility, purity and patience, endowed with the dowry of faith, hope, and charity, which take us immediately to God.

Furthermore, he who obeys is easily victorious over the world. The world says that he who excels is great. He who obeys proves that he does not listen to him, the seducer, at all. By facts he proves that there is greater glory in obeying everyone, superiors as well as inferiors or equals, when by office they have been appointed to command. What else can the world still do against an obedient Christian?

The devil obtains even less. Satan is able to bring someone to ruin easily because he is able to easily deceive him. Yet it is impossible that one who is truly obedient can be deceived by anyone. It is true, as it is true that God exists, that he who obeys his superior, obeys God himself. Did you ever hear that by obeying God the devil can ever seduce anyone? As long as Adam and Eve obeyed the Lord, they had dominion over the earth. They became slaves, and vile slaves indeed, when, by disobeying God, they began to listen to the deceitful discourses of Satan.

4. For now you can rejoice with the saints and the angels in heaven. You can ask them to rejoice with you, because God has given you the grace to obtain such a great victory. You can rejoice for it also with others, when by manifesting the glories of Christian obedience we may become a source of edification for others. Yet let us be very careful: there are so many who are excellent teachers in

speaking about the values of obedience, yet they are not capable of practicing any act worth of noble example.

What good is it to preach by words, if first we do not prepare our soul with example? Jesus Christ, who is the holiness by essence, began by practicing those virtues which he wanted to instill into the hearts of men. Since he knew that example counts more than words, he spent thirty years in displaying the practice of obedience, limiting himself to three years in explaining his lessons on submission.

I bring my teaching on this subject to you through this homily. May heaven be pleased if I can do it by giving an example all my entire life. Let us pray that both I, the shepherd, and you, the faithful, will one day be able to sing with heavenly joy: "We have obeyed, therefore we are victorious."

REFLECTIONS

1. A glorious victory is the victory of obedience by which a Christian wins over his senses.
2. This is a victory that surpasses every other victory.
3. This victory presumes every great virtue in the heart of man.
4. Because of obedience, one has the right to rejoice with the angels of heaven and with his fellow men here below, for the purpose of giving them a good example.

GOSPEL OF THE SECOND SUNDAY
AFTER EPIPHANY

A fleeting shadow

1. A traveler who climbs the ridges of the Alps during the summer season may see a strange gigantic figure grow thick all around himself, walking in front by excessively long steps. The expedient mountaineer does not worry about this figure. He looks up and says: "I know you are the shadow of a passing cloud." Thus my time here below goes by. So why care for earthly pleasures? Thus passes away the journey of my life; what does it matter that I have to bear with days of some kind of tribulations?

We read in the holy Gospel that a young couple, poor but confident in divine Providence, felt being called to join in the mutual lifelong commitment of marriage. Like travelers who do not waste time other than for due rest, they gathered around themselves for the day of their marriage their close relatives, and their trusty friends. They sat down to savor the bread of their cordial friendship, but at the highpoint of their frugal meal they ran out of wine.

Mary and Jesus happened to sit at the table of that good couple. The virgin Mary turned to her son and whispered in his ear: "They have no more wine." Jesus answered her: "The hour to work miracles has not yet come." Nonetheless Mary signaled to the servants and said: "Do whatever Jesus tells you." The divine Savior commanded them: "Fill up with water the jars and then draw from them and serve it at the table." The servants obeyed and served so good a wine that all the guests marveled about it.[1]

The first ones who enjoyed it were the groom and the bride who, without omitting whatever belonged to their simple and religious customs, did not stop from repeating the maxim from the *Book of Proverbs* that says: "For who knows what is good for a man in life, the limited days of his vain life (which God has made like a shadow)?"[2] What a wise thought that should be in the back of our mind all the time. The time of this life is a fleeting shadow. Why, then, should one spend time and energies for the fleeting apparition of a figure that quickly vanishes?

2. Consider a wise father who suggests to his son what needs to be done on that day. The son is a young man who is capable of work, yet he is not immune from his defects of rashness and fiery nature. See. The father tells him: "Go to that far away field and follow this route that I'm showing you. I know that this is longer, nonetheless it is the safest one. Once you arrive there, begin immediately harvesting and keep going slowly until the evening. Tomorrow I will assign other jobs to you, and then others, so that you may grow in your career."

The young man nods indicating with his head that he intends to obey punctually, yet in his heart he thinks to act more quickly following his own judgment. Look at him. He rushes to the field as if he were pursued, takes the shortest paths which are dangerous, faltering all along, wasting time and losing patience. He finally reaches the field when the sun is already high on the horizon. Then he puts his hands on a

---

[1] Jn 2:1-10
[2] Eccl 6:12

type of scythe that is not the recommended one for harvesting, going through the field with desperate frenzy. He sweats profusely but he does not rest, because he wants to achieve a job greater than what was assigned to him by his father. The evening comes and he can barely stand on his feet. The father sees the confusion of the work done and the waste of wheat scattered all around. He sees his son fall sick into his arms and with regret says: "What does it matter to you, young man, to want to perform a job greater than the one that was assigned to you?"

There are many who resemble that thoughtless yet dear young man. God has put them in a certain condition, yet they long for a higher one. In the name of God the superior has commanded them to accept and carry out a certain ministry, yet they do not accept it at all. They aspire for greater things. They want tasks, they want devout tasks. They rush through the tasks imposed on them, thereby carrying them out badly, under the pretext that they want to fulfill more relevant tasks.

What do you say about it? Is there more than one among you who has reason for blaming himself for such a defect? Certainly, all those who are ambitious seek things which they do not have, since they belong to the future. And since they belong to the future, how do you know whether they are for your soul's advantage or damage?

3. It is worthwhile to reflect upon this. A traveler who has a long way to go, does not stop to look at the enchanting gardens, golden palaces, or at the street embellished with flowers. He says to himself: "I have to be at my destination before dark." Our thinking should be similar to this. Only one thing is necessary, to save one's soul. To save one's soul all energies available must be employed. This is business of

utmost importance to which every business of material interest must yield.

We have a journey to complete. Who cares for looking around or even stopping here and there if all along we lose the path that takes us safely to our homeland? The philosopher says: *"Age quod agis (Pay attention to what you are doing)"* Concentrate on what you are doing, so that you may perform it with perfection. We have to give an account to God our Father for the tasks he entrusts to us. He will never ask us for things we have taken upon us on our own will rather than upon a specific request from heaven.

4. Let us not waste time, for after all by how many years can we extend our life on earth? Would you think that you may reach one hundred years? We have spent too many already! Who can assure us that we are going to live for a few more days? Given that we are going to live for a dozen more years, how long is it in comparison with the centuries of eternity? It is only a matter of days. Do we think that a few days are too many for preparing ourselves for the journey to eternity, thereby we spend so much a part of them in planning, in aspirations, and worldly vanities?

5. Do we realize that time slips away? Time flies faster than the shot of an arrow, faster than the flight of any bird. It flies even faster than the flash of the lightning. As a matter of fact it goes so fast that we do not even realize. It happens that we linger on conversing in the public square, while others are enjoying themselves watching a comedy. There you see on the wall the sun-dial signaling the hours by its shadow. The shadow moves so slowly that you do not realize that it moves, yet are you aware of how much the earth has rotated around the sun to signal that movement slight as it might be? In one

hour the earth has traveled millions of kilometers. How swift time is in its way! Yet we do not even pay attention to it!

Diligence is required of us. Let us pay attention so as not to waste one single moment of time. Let us take it away from conversations, sleep, meals. When there is a shortage of iron, wheat or anything else, we have to keep a close check on them. In times of siege even water is rationed, cheap as it might be, because there is not much of it. Very brief is the time of our pilgrimage here below. Let us hasten to fulfill our journey so as to enter that homeland where our common Father may reward us for the faithful services we have rendered along our journey here below.

REFLECTIONS

1. A fleeting shadow is the time that passes on.
2. We need to perform our task well, without wasting time longing for a higher post.
3. Who knows whether a higher position would benefit us or not?
4. Time is so brief.
5. It flies like a shadow, without one even realizing its passage.

GOSPEL OF THE THIRD SUNDAY
AFTER EPIPHANY

Thick gloom of darkness

1. A traveler may easily find shelter from an imminent storm in a home. Yet it is rare that a son, whom everyone knows has run away from his father's house for not being willing to obey him, finds compassion in it.

We learn from the Gospel that Jesus cured a leper, and that he also listened to the prayer of the centurion for curing his servant. In doing so, we know that he used very frightening words. Because of his great faith, the centurion deserved to be praised by the divine Savior before everyone. Yet, the very same Redeemer, after stating, "I have never found this much faith in Israel," added: "Many will come from the east and west and will find a place at the banquet in the kingdom of God with Abraham, Isaac, and Jacob, while the natural heirs of the kingdom will be driven out into the dark. Wailing will be heard there, and the grinding of teeth."[1]

Miserable punishment! The Lord is in our midst, the chosen son of heaven, the privileged son of a pious mother, the holy Church. Yet it is painful to think of this: how many are still here, in our Italy, who do not believe in Jesus at all, or who deny belief in the very existence of God in heaven! The Supreme Pontiff who has been governing the Church of Jesus Christ for the past five years recently stated: "Individuals educated to hate religion and allowed to grow at

---

[1] Mt 8:1-13

39

their pleasure in all kind of boldness and audaciousness, carry out their iniquitous attempts. There are newspapers that spread around impiety freely and with impunity, curse and blaspheme the holiest things, hurl insults and offenses at God himself, and, horrible thing to say, extol Satan."[1]

How horrible! As St. Jude the Apostle says, these are the ones for whom the thick gloom of darkness has been reserved forever.[2] Let us ponder on the lightning of the punishment prepared for those who do not believe, and besides not envying the lot of those wretched ones, let us regard them with indulgence from the bottom of our heart.

2. Think of a day in an unsettled season, when the weather is cold and rainy, and the storms frequent and floody. A young man decides to climb the Alps, and is determined to reach all the peaks. The farmers down in the plain try to dissuade him, the pros list to him all the dangers, to no avail. The young man climbs recklessly, when suddenly clouds come in like giants covering the whole summit of the mountain, rolling down the cliffs and causing strong winds that soon turn into a violent storm. All along a deluge of rain and hail falls, with claps of thunder and flashs of lightning that shake the mountain and split the rocks with roars. The wretched young man is there. Enveloped all around in darkness he does not know which rock or reef to hold on to for safety. In his mind he feels the darkness of a distressing regret, with no help from anybody. Who is going to feel bad for that wretched one who came to ruin of his own will?

---

[1] Pope Leo XIII was elected on February 20, 1878, and therefore these words quoted by the author should go back to 1883. This passage, however, seems to hint on themes developed also in the encyclical letter *Humanum genus* of April 20, 1884.

[2] Jd 13

Likewise punishment will be experienced in hell by those who did not want to believe in God who was speaking to them. They will be surrounded by the darkness of hell, thicker and more palpable than the darkness which enveloped Egypt during the famous ten plagues. They, also, will feel darkness within themselves. They will say: "We could have saved ourselves, yet we did not want to be saved!"

3. The exterior darkness will be very thick. Imagine a very deep cave, surrounded by immense walls of dirt, with no opening of light whatsoever: this is the pit of hell.

Imagine now in it a pile of corpses, that are so tight that a finger cannot be moved nor the eye blink. This is the state of the damned who at the last judgment were condemned to be in hell piled up in body and soul, as it is written in the prophet Isaiah: *"Calcavi eos in furore meo - I trod them in my anger."* [1]

Finally, we find in the *Book of Revelation* how down in the bottom there is a fiery pool of burning sulphur, that is, *stagnum ignis ardentis sulphure.* [2] This pool of burning sulphur sends out balls of fire, all surrounded by whirling spirals of smoke. The smoke rises above, but, unable to come out, comes down again to reinforce more misty smoke coming up. There will be no end to that whirling gloom, which is referred to by the above-mentioned apostle.

What a benefit for me and you so far since we have not fallen into that gloom! Yet, how much do we care about not falling into it at our death?

---

[1] Is 63:3
[2] Rv 19:20

4. Worse still is the gloom of mind. Think of a soul highly vexed by scruples or aridity. What a terrible suffering! The poor souls think: "Who knows if I will be saved!", and thus their limbs shake all over. The damned will tremble even more. Down there they will see clearly that there is no longer a ray of hope for them. They are damned and so they will be forever. God will no more bend with compassion over them.

This causes a gloom in the souls of the damned, a gloom of despair in mind and heart. Their passions of anger, blasphemy, and iniquity rekindle ever more, thereby producing the kind of blindness we are talking about. Add to it the atrocious torments of hell. Even here on earth when a pain is so intense in one's body, it might cause a great distress. The poor infirmed person does nothing but moan: "It hurts, it hurts", and thinks only of that.

What horrible gloom will that be! It is less perceived than the physical blindness, for it is a moral darkness, yet since it affects one's soul, it is more tormenting.

5. Were that darkness transient, as a storm, though impetuous, is transient here on earth! Still, do not even let a thought cross your mind that gloom will cease in hell even for a single moment for all eternity. It lasts for ever.

He who is sick and cannot close his eyes during the night, awaits the light of the new day, which finally enters in through the window-panes. In hell a dark night follows on another, and so on and on without end. What a fright just thinking of it!

6. That gloom is reserved for all those who did not want to open their eyes to the light of truth. Do you realize now what great evil it is not to listen to God who speaks? Furthermore, would you like to know whether you will be

42

able to enjoy the light of paradise or bear with the eternal gloom of hell? Take a look at yourselves. If you are eager to listen to whatever pertains to God and paradise, you have a sign that you love the light and that light will cause you to rejoice one day. However, if you flee the light as much as you can, to listen to and follow the demands of the evil passion more than the light of reason and truth, then fear that the horrible gloom of darkness which we have considered today may not overtake you.

REFLECTIONS

1. A gloom of darkness.
2. The infernal pit.
3. The damned piled up there.
4. The darkness of mind.
5. This gloom of darkness is eternal.
6. Reserved for those who always wanted to keep their eyes closed to the light of truth.

GOSPEL OF THE FOURTH SUNDAY
AFTER EPIPHANY

In time of war

1. Man opens his eyes to the light of the day, finds himself in a battlefield and utters a cry of sorrow. He will never stop that cry until his last day of life. All along you hear: "Life is a battle!" Miserable are those men who have to enlist forever in the army.

The apostles of the divine Savior lived with Jesus, nevertheless they were not out of the battlefield. We read in today's Gospel how, upon entering a little boat in order to cross the lake, Jesus felt asleep, when suddenly such a violent storm came up on the lake that the apostles feared drowning. They cried out piteously: "Lord, save us for we are lost!" To them Jesus said: "How little faith you have! Don't you realize that you have the Savior with you?" Then, to the sea he said: "Calm down!" Complete calm ensued.[1]

The danger of the apostles is our danger as well, the support of the apostles is also our support. Here we are on earth, on a battlefield. Holy Job said it too: "Is not man's life on earth a drudgery?"[2] We are living in time of war. What are we expected to do under those conditions?

2. Let us take a look at the field of Catholic battle. Behold the standard: it is the sign of the cross. Behold the weapons aii arranged in a beautiful order: they are holy

---

[1] Mt 8:23-27
[2] Jb 7:1

Sacraments, prayer, pious works. The enemies being fought are the evil appetites.

Let us go into the battle. Here we have one of the two: we either win or die. The winner receives paradise as a reward. The loser receives hell as a punishment. Do you care for winning so that you may be triumphant? Hear what I am going to tell you how a Christian soldier must act in time of war.

3. We are battling on an open field. Don't think that you can take it easy at your pleasure, that you can have a good time and relax as you please. How can this be done in time of war? Hannibal had overcome incredible obstacles on his way from Africa to the very gates of Rome, yet once he reached the plains of Capua, he wanted to relax during the winter season. Sweet leisure of that pleasant climate! Thus he lost in a few days what he had conquered with much sacrifice of time and people and was forced to return to his country, defeated and embarassed.

Let us be convinced of this: in time of war one does not attend a comedy entertainment. Since this war lasts through our entire life, it is true that as long as we live, we are expected to struggle.

4. We are at war. There are many Christians who want to be rewarded here on earth. Yet when did anyone hear that a reward is given while a battle is going on strong? Reward is given once the battle is over.

You pray but you find no consolation in it. You do a good deed and you get tribulations and disturbances as a result. You do things that benefit others and you get much ungratefulness from them. You work hard, yet you don't get out of poverty. Why do you complain anyway? Listen to this.

A general, who knows well how to lead his soldiers, risks his most valiant men in the greatest dangers, since he knows that they long for the most noteworthy rewards. Take courage by looking up to paradise since in heaven we will be given the reward that is appropriate to the struggle sustained.

5. We are in times of battle. Who does not know that at time of battle all soldiers must obey their captain faithfully? Furthermore, they are expected to obey not only in easy things but also in difficult things. Think for a moment. Even when the captain raises the whip to punish, a soldier is expected to submit respectfully. There is no obedience in our world greater than the obedience in the army. If a soldier opposes his commanders, he is sent to jail or even punished with death.

One more obligation on our part: we have to obey blindly. A soldier is not allowed to question whether the commands given by his captain are more or less appropriate. His duty is to obey blindly. Now, see whether or not you have any good reason when in acting you think you can follow your whims. In time of battle one commands and all the others obey.

6. We are in time of battle. Who ever considered himself safe as long as the battle was going on? There are always ambushes to guard against, there are always assaults to counteract in spiritual battle. The ambushes are the snares of the devil which you can attentively detect. The assaults, then, are the clear and blatant aggressions which come from the world, or the devil, or the flesh. These assaults are very common every day. It is good, then, that we are in fear every day. It doesn't pay here to be a veteran or a recruit. Perfect Christians have less to fear than newly become Christians, for

it is a fact that as long as man lives here on earth, he risks damnation. Consequently, in time of war who can be safe? Safer is the one who fears more, striving to protect himself from danger.

7. We are on a battlefield. There are some people who consider themselves saints for having battled for a while. Watch it! What is warfare? It is a testing time. In battle a soldier is tested to see whether he is a valiant or a vile soldier. To make a safer judgment in this regard it is good to wait until the battle is over. Never think too much of yourself. As long as you undergo a battle you can never be too experienced. God will reward you at the end. If you boast about it first, you run the risk of losing the reward for the sufferings which you have borne daily.

8. We are on a battlefield. No soldier is allowed to take his life in order to avoid a fight. Whoever is suspected of doing so is declared infamous. After many years of service he is allowed to be discharged from the army. As a matter of fact, when a soldier has gone through many afflictions, he can justly ask for discharge.

There are Christians who consider taking their life in order not to battle. Most vile Christians! Whoever does so will be given the infamy of hell. However, a Christian who finds himself afflicted by extraordinary struggle, can ask God to come out of this situation on earth. Even Job made such a request to the Lord, even though he was a very patient man. An individual who says that asking such a thing from God would be a sign of weakness, would give the idea that he is very strong, even though he has not battled one single day as a valiant one.

At this point I want to add no more helpful advice. I have discussed what could be helpful in conducting yourselves. We are on a battlefield. You have understood what needs to be done in time of warfare.

REFLECTIONS

1. We are in time of warfare.
2. Let us take a look at the battlefield.
3. There is no time nor place of rest, but struggle.
4. The reward is given not here below, but in heaven.
5. On a battlefield it is good to obey.
6. And keep watch, for the dangers are continuous.
7. As long as one is in battle, he can perish.
8. He who is afflicted by weariness, must ask for the permission to be relieved from it.

GOSPEL OF THE FIFTH SUNDAY AFTER EPIPHANY

In a Christian society

1. Speaking of the Christian community, the apostles of the divine Savior call it a holy nation, a people he claims for his own.[1] They refer to the individual Christians as children of the Lord, living temples of the Holy Spirit, sharers themselves of the divinity[2], since they are enriched with grace and the Sacraments of Jesus Christ.

Nonetheless it is not true that every single individual is a saint. The Divine Savior himself compared his Church to a field in which the farmer sowed good seed. However, his enemy came and sowed weeds. Naturally both wheat and weeds grew together. The owner lets both of them grow, but at the harvest time the wheat only is gathered in the barns of the heavenly Father. The weeds are, instead, gathered to be burned.[3]

In Christian society good people are mingled with evil people. In truth, the evil individuals often vex the good ones, yet, while they persecute good people, they give them a chance to perfect themselves further. Nonetheless, it is a shame that in a society of saints more than one traitor can be found, more than one murderer, as well as more than one fraudulent person and one liar! Realizing that the apostle St. Peter felt very bad about it and begged Christians by saying:

---

[1] 1 Pt 2: 9
[2] See 1 Cor 3:16; 2 Pt 1:4
[3] See Mt 13:14-30

49

"See to it that none of you suffers for being a murderer, a thief, a malefactor, or a destroyer of another's rights. If anyone suffers for being a Christian, however, he ought not to be ashamed."[1] Let us reflect upon this request of the apostle, piece by piece, and let us strive to adhere to it intimately.

2. Think of a house that is assaulted by thieves who want to plunder it, by assassins who want to slaughter its inhabitants, by dishonest individuals who plan to desecrate its parts, and by other people who want to put it on fire. All these wicked people exert great effort to carry out their evil intent. How abominable they are! Everyone is going to cry out against them to be exterminated.

At the same time a band of chosen pious individuals gather, facing all dangers in order to save that house. They attack the assassins to free the inhabitants of the house from death, and assault those furious dishonest individuals to prevent them from bringing scandal and grievance into that house in words and deeds. Those good people finally disperse the evil ones who intended to put that house on fire. Blessed may they be for rushing to help! In a few moments they save that neighborhood from a terrible infestation. They suffered for showing courage, but now everyone applauds them, while those brothers of theirs whom they have saved, fall at their feet.

How dear is the presence of Christians filled with charity who strive to do good to others with all their strength! The apostle prays that the followers of the Savior may be just that. The others are not worthy of the name they carry. Dear apostle of the Lord, we promise you, we will listen to the voice of your imploring requests.

---

[1] 1 Pt 4:15-16

50

3. Let us now consider the heart of St. Raymond, or St. Augustine, and of many others who, in order to save their brothers from death, offered themselves to be jailed, ready to suffer all sufferings. Let us consider the heart of St. Charles Borromeo or St. Jerome Emiliani and of so many others who reduced themselves to squalid poverty in order to relieve human miseries. St. Vincent De Paul one day went to the government of France to defend the requests of the poor. St. John of God threw himself into the midst of flames in order to save poor infirmed people from death.

Faithful servants of the Lord, in order to follow Jesus Christ crucified, they must bear with being derided by men, maltreated by persecutors, offended by adversaries. What are these little wretched people going to do? The apostle St. Peter is very discreet in giving regulations on this matter. He says: "You are allowed to feel bad about it, yet you are not supposed to be ashamed of it." One can feel bad about it, for it is barely possible that the senses do not resent it. Yet we must not be ashamed of it, for one is not a true disciple of Christ if he feels ashamed of him. What would you say about an individual who is ashamed of his father and denies him?

4. On the contrary, the apostle calls us to glorify Jesus Christ through suffering. This can be achieved in two ways. Suppose two brothers who have received the same, very serious, wrong from one of the members of their family. One of them says: "Be patient!" and shows to be willing to forgive. The second brother not only does forgive with all his heart, but he even embraces his wrongdoing brother, invites him for dinner and finally gives to him the best of his belongings. This is the way St. Charles and St. Francis acted in regard to the assassins who attempted to take their lives. Thus St. Ciprian, at the very act of being beheaded, made his

executioner heir of whatever he still possessed. Most noble example that will never be erased from the memory of men, benefited as well as edified! Thus one gives to the Lord the most beautiful glory possible.

This is an example to be followed, not the example of Christians who, when unjustly treated, call for punishment from heaven. Never pray that God may punish sinners! When the apostles went to Jesus to tell him: "Send down fire from heaven, because the people of Samaria did not listen to us", the divine Savior answered: "You do not know what you are asking for... you do not know what evil spirit is leading you. My will is not to lose men, but to save them." To pray for those who speak ill of us, to do good to those who do wrong to us, this is the true character of a good Christian. Let us all do that and we will give glory to the Lord.

REFLECTIONS

1. In Christian society there is the wheat of the good and the weeds of the evil ones.
2. Two opposite fields around a house.
3. In defending the ways of Christ one can regret, but never be ashamed of it.
4. We must glorify God according to the name of Christians that we carry.

GOSPEL OF THE SIXTH SUNDAY AFTER EPIPHANY

Where there is a will there is a way

1. Worldly people frequently praise those illustrious individuals who, by their determination, grew in their reputation in matters of arts or humanities, philosophy or politics. People dedicated to religion not only praise but even exalt their beloved brothers and sisters who, by remaining attached to God intimately, progressed illustriously in the Church of the Lord, instruments of providence for the holiness of all Christians. St. Paul the Apostle, who was so daring in his undertakings, said: "I have the strength for everything through him who empowers me."[1]

In today's Gospel we read as follows: "Jesus proposed another parable to them and said: 'The kingdom of heaven is like a mustard seed that a person took and sowed in a field. It is the smallest of all the seeds, yet when fully grown it is the largest of plants. It becomes a large bush, and the birds of the sky come and dwell in its branches.' He spoke to them another parable: 'The kingdom of heaven is like yeast that a woman took and mixed with three measures of wheat flour until the whole batch was leavened.' All these things Jesus spoke to the crowds in parables, to fulfill what had been said through the prophet: 'I will open my mouth in parables, I will announce what has been hidden from the foundation of the world.'"[2]

---

[1] Phil 4:13
[2] Mt 13:31-35

See, then, in the holy Gospel two very dear parables that prove how much a Christian individual can do in the Church of Jesus Christ. A tiny seed of good grows into a tree of deeds; a handful of yeast of good example ferments a mass of bread, that is the multitude of faithful who prepare themselves to enter paradise. Our outcome will certainly be different from the outcome of those who follow the world. We can indeed say that when there is a will there is a way! By God's grace everything is possible to a Christian. Let us take a look into it with all our reasoning abilities.

2. We have seen how simple fishermen have become apostles, how uneducated people have been able to turn pagan individuals into followers of Jesus Christ. We have seen simple children and modest young ladies break the power and fierceness of Roman tyrants. We have seen how simple-minded farmers grow into popes and make the iniquitous tremble. We have seen simple women from the populace sought by princes and popes for assistance and advice.

Do we wonder, then, why St. Paul the apostle said: *"Omnia possum in eo qui me comfortat - I have the strength for everything in him who empowers me."* God is our father and he is the almighty. What cannot a well-bred son do when he is tied with love to his excellent father? In Christianity where there is a will there is a way. With God's help everything is possible. Open wide the two eyes you have in your forehead. Look at the host of powerful people who take care of you and then dare not to put greater trust in the power and grace of the Most High!

3. The Apostle indeed set the sustenance to act. When the Spirit descended upon the Apostles, these were transformed from timid individuals into courageous ones,

from ignorant to wise ones. The power of God acted like a giant with a pigmy who wants to move a mountain, transferring into him his own strength so that the pigmy can afterward cooperate.

I'm going to give you a few examples. When Moses was shepherding his father-in-law's sheep, who could have said that he was going to be the savior of his people crossing the Red Sea?... And thinking of the young David playing with his pasturing sheep, who could have claimed: "This boy will win over the giant Goliath and will later become the king of Israel"?... No one foresaw Samson's strength... no one could have thought of the miracles of Gideon or Joshua. When Elijah, Elisha or Jeremiah and other prophets were children, no one would have claimed that they would be able to foresee the future, or would have threatened the wicked, or chastised the powerful for their iniquities. Yet they did so because God assisted them.

When years ago the mother of John Maria Mastai Ferretti saw her six-year old son drowning in the rushing river and later on seriously sick at the age of fifteen, then apopletic at the age of twenty-two, could his parents and relatives as well have imagined that he was going to become a pope? Nonetheless he became a pope, and he was a great one, the angelic pope who was excellently pious in his behaviour, and Pius even by name.

Consequently let us have confidence and comfort one another. The Lord is the one who is going to assist us. With God's help a Christian can do everything. If others were able to achieve magnificent goals all over the world, will we not be able to obtain more in carrying out with perfection other undertakings which are so minor and particularly attached to our state in life and to the simplicity of a family? Brothers and sisters, let us think of this with holy joy: for a Christian, where there is the will, there is a way. The limits of possibilities and power for a Christian are marked by the power and the grace of the Almighty.

4. Furthermore, God grants this power and this grace according to our cooperation. When a little boy struggles in trying to roll a big rock which he can barely move, he is quickly helped by his father. Yet his father would not make a move if he did not see his son make the attempt so eagerly.

Here I give you a few examples. St. Teresa was so eager to reform her order of Carmelites. How many prayers did she make to God and how lovingly did she sigh! All along she heartily sought the assistance of the powerful of the world. As a reward for her good will God granted that St. Teresa eventually achieved her goal, which was certainly a huge one.

St. Dominic wished to be able to stop the very serious evils which afflicted the Church in his times because of the enemies of peace. What did he do? Not content with just wishing in his heart, he went to church, knelt before the image of Mary and said: "One of the two, O Blessed Mother: help me to defeat the enemies of faith, or I will stay here before you until I die." This heartfelt wish of St. Dominic pleased the Most High, and the pious religious was heard so as to succeed in defeating the heretics with the prayer of the holy rosary.

See how an ardent heart becomes strong. The Lord revealed to more than one of his faithful servants: "I give my heart to him who gives his heart to me." You understand me, then. If you desire to do more for the glory of the Lord, have confidence in God and give on your part the best of your efforts.

5. Under those terms you will experience the effect of divine grace. Will you be tried by vexations, wrongs and insults? You will bear them willingly. Will you be affected by privations, hunger, thirst, heat or cold? By God's grace you will bear with them. Didn't people like you, made of fragilities, bear with them, too?

Take for example St. Charles Borromeo. Noble by birth, sickly and frail, still he endured pains due to traveling, studies, pastoral visitations and preaching. He underwent fastings, vigils and sufferings, until like the image of suffering met with the image of terror, the pestilence in the city of Milan. Then, he seemed to rejuvenate and did so many and such great things recorded in history as true, things that puzzle the mind of man. So prodigious in number and variety were the undertakings of Archbishop Borromeo! Questioning that fearless man, one would be told: "Why wonder?... Man can do everything with God's assistance."

As a result, my dear Christians, I am very well convinced that I have given you some help for the undertakings of your life. Believe it for ever: with God's help one can do whatever he wills. With this good thought in our mind, let us all set ourselves to carry out those works of good which in so evil times God and the Church of Jesus Christ expect of each one of us.

REFLECTIONS

1. Where there is a will, there is a way.
2. In the Church of the Lord a wretched individual can grow into an illustrious and worthy member of Christian society.
3. The help comes from heaven.
4. The Christian gives his cooperation.
5. With this alone he can overcome all difficulties.

GOSPEL OF SEPTUAGESIMA SUNDAY

Christian battling

1. As a matter of fact you see how man has to battle here on earth every day of his life. Every day has its toil. One has to toil manually, another mentally, another emotionally. The sentence was given already six thousand years ago: "You will live with the sweat of your brow."[1] Work, however, is a blessing. We see it ourselves. By working we make up for a good part for the damages caused by our sin, while idleness makes it worse consistently.

We read in the holy Gospel how various laborers were in the square at different hours. Some at the first hour, others at the third, sixth and ninth, and others at the eleventh hour. An excellent landowner went out at all hours and told them: "Go into my vineyard and work, and I will give you a just wage." The laborers went to work joyfully. When evening came, all of them received the same wage agreed upon by the laborers of the first hour. Those who had worked all day grumbled, but the landowner said to them: "Money is mine: cannot I give it as I like? Didn't I pay you the wage agreed upon?"[2]

We all have to work. Let us work at the time and the manner God assigns to us. This is our battle. St. Paul himself, writing to the faithful of Corinth, said: "Thus I do not run aimlessly; I do not fight as if I were shadowboxing. No, I

---

[1] Gen 3:19
[2] Mt 20:1-16

drive my body and train it, for fear that, after having preached to others, I myself should not be disqualified."[1] With these words the Apostle points out two things: the battlefield assigned to us, and how organized it must be.

2. Our battle is a journey that does not end until we have reached the summit of the mountain of perfection that God wants us to reach. All along we have to pay attention to the fact that, for us to reach the goal, God sets certain means of virtue to sustain us, and expects us to fight certain evil habits and vices. The means of assistance of virtues are like the assistance of a blessed angel, the weight of vices is like the effort of many devils who hang around waiting for us to fall. Let us look at these figures of virtue or vice. To which virtues are we more inclined? Mercy or justice? Patience or severity?

Let us act in comformity to the vocation to which God has called us. The Lord grants many graces to his people: to one he grants the spirit of meekness, to another the spirit of fear, of tears, or of chastity, or of any of the many gifts of the Holy Spirit. Now it is up to us to be able to ascertain which among those angels we must accompany in a special way, and stick to him with all the affection possible.

Likewise there are figures of devils, which we have to avoid. The devils which we have to fight are all the abominable vices. Some of these might assault us with rage. Concupiscence is an unrestrained beast that disturbs most of us. After this and along with it come the passions of anger, envy, pride or greed, as well as the seven furies of hell that, out of anger, come out of the abyss to ruin souls.

---

[1] 1 Cor 9:26

Let us ponder upon them, and in a special way let us pay attention to the one which stands above all others so that we can fight it with greater ardor. To that bloody beast let us oppose all our energies of heavenly virtues, our arrows of divine power. Then, pushing it back into the abyss, let us say: "You are not allowed to ruin a follower of the Savior; you who have been a liar and murderer since the beginning, hide into your hell." With such firmness acted Sts. Anthony, Macharius, Ilarion, and Paul in the desert. With similar faith the confessors and virgins hasten to the cities, and thus they reach a safe place.

3. The way to which the Apostle was called was the way of preaching; the weapon to achieve his goal was his zeal along with the mortification of his body. Truly the Apostle looked at this mortification as the heavenly guide to precede him in his journeys. As a matter of fact, he points out how he punished his body, beating it up to the point of sores and bloodshed. Holy Apostle! After sustaining so many toils, besides enduring so many journeys and overcoming so many dangers, wasn't it appropriate for him to take care of his body so as to spare it for the sake of so many people? Not at all! He believed that the mortification of his body would be the only means to save the world. What do we think we are? Perhaps, more necessary for the world than Paul in preaching the Gospel?

4. Furthermore, notice one more good reason why St. Paul punished his body. He punished it out of fear, for after saving so many others, he wouldn't be lost himself. This is what the Apostle feared. If that holy preacher feared, how much more should we, who are much less than he, that is miserable sinners!

If we have done some good, has an angel come down from heaven to tell us that we will be saved? Certainly we are not sure, and since we are not, how fearful should we be! After all, we are going to be happy or unhappy forever. Forever in heaven or with Lucifer in hell. With such a doubt, light as it might be, but certainly fatal in regard to its result, how can we be living so happily?

5. Do you think that concupiscence is completely extinct in you? It was not even extinct in St. Paul the Apostle! Concupiscence is present even in perfect individuals, and it lasts until the end. It is certainly felt by Christians who are still imperfect.

Thus you should conclude: the Apostle St. Paul who had converted such a great part of the world, he who had mastered his body consistently, was in fear, and you feel so secure? Think, at least, that concupiscence is a venom that is formed and remains within you. A sick or evil heart stirs it up. You have a danger of death in your own home. In the case of a wicked end, you are the one who procures your own ruin. May heaven spare us, may heaven spare us! Are we expected to fight it? We will fight fiercely. In the meantime the order to be followed is this: we have to watch ourselves in a special way while we try to do good to others. Now and always we have to mortify in a special way our body so that our spirit may triumph.

REFLECTIONS

1. Christian battle.
2. Christian battle consists in our journey to the mountain of perfection to which God calls us.
3. It is helpful in this journey that we chastise the flesh.
4. Fearing that we are damned while we try to do something good for others.
5. The wicked stimulus of iniquity resides within our own heart.

GOSPEL OF SEXAGESIMA SUNDAY

A remedy not to die

1. The people of the world claim that they have found remedies for all evils, yet they confess that they have not found any remedy against the evil of death. Death comes by more furiously and exterminates more assiduously. The Lord of heaven, instead, shows us a remedy that prevents us from dying forever. It is God who assures us of this and there is no reason for you to doubt. This remedy consists in listening to and then carrying out faithfully the word of the Lord. As we read in St. John's Gospel, Jesus says as follows: "Amen, amen, I say to you, whoever keeps my word will never see death."[1] Did you understand? It is Jesus, the wisdom of the Eternal Father, who speaks and swears to tell the truth.

The divine Savior himself in today's Gospel says as follows: "A sower went out to sow his seed. And as he sowed, some seed fell on the path and was trampled, and the birds of the sky ate it up. Some fell on rocky ground, and when it grew, it withered for lack of moisture. Some seed fell among thorns, and the thorns grew up and choked it. And some seed fell on good soil, and when it grew, it produced fruit a hundredfold." Jesus explained the parable, then, and said: "The seed is the word of God. Those on the path are the ones who have heard, but the devil comes and takes away the word from their hearts that they may not believe and be saved. Those on rocky ground are the ones who, when they hear, receive the word with joy, but they have no root; they

---

[1] Jn 8:51

63

believe only for a time and fall away in time of trial. As for the seed that fell among thorns, they are the ones who have heard, but as they go along, they are choked by the anxieties and riches and pleasures of life, and they fail to produce mature fruit. But as for the seed that fell on rich soil, they are the ones who, when they have heard the word, embrace it with a generous and good heart, and bear fruit through perseverance."[1]

The fruit of the word of the Lord is like the fruit of the tree of life in the garden of Eden. He who eats of its fruit will never die. Let us ponder upon this truth for it is very consoling.

2. Suppose that in summertime two individuals, very different from each other in regard to personality and background, climb a mountain: one is an uneducated shepherd and the other is a learned botanist. You can easily see how the uneducated shepherd steps with his feet and hits with his stick all kinds of grass, since he is not able to distinguish one from the others. The botanist, instead, stops here and there, tip-toeing in wonder, then bends down with joy to pull from this and that grass, bundling them all together, and takes them to his laboratory to make good use of them.

Think now of people of two different types as they approach the word of the Lord. There are people who do not distinguish the sayings of the Gospel from those told by any philosopher, thus they read the passages from Scriptures as they read a text from history, science or from any other writer. These people are ignorant or evil. More probably they are bad Christians, or at least indifferent Christians, who confuse heavenly interests with the miserable things of this

---

[1] Lk 8: 4-15

earth. Then there are Christians, and by God's mercy they are still many, who accurately make a distinction concerning every heavenly maxim, meditate upon it, save it in their hearts and cherish it more than any treasure on earth.

Brothers and sisters, to which category do we belong? Let us reflect upon it seriously, because it is said that the word of God is the source of eternal life. How can one expect not to ever die when he is not willing to make use of the only remedy required for it?

3. All the while it is very true that he who listens to the word of the Lord will never die. He will neither die in body nor in his soul. He will not die in his body because, although even the just must die physically, actually his death is not a true death but only a fortunate transition. The body will dwell in the grave for a little while and then it will rise gloriously into heaven. Jesus Christ himself died, yet see him gloriously coming back to life on the third day. The farmer sows his seeds to rot in the soil, yet he does not feel bad about it because he knows that it soon will grow into golden wheat.

What dies is the body of the damned. This in fact will be buried lower from its earthly grave into the abyss of hell, where it will not die but live only to experience all and forever the agonies of death. The soul of the damned also suffers. That is not the case of the just. In fact, while he does not die in his body, even less he will die in his soul. The divine word is the remedy to never die.

You can see how one dies of old age, or of a disease, of sudden death or even because of a fall off a cliff. The soul can die because of lack of spiritual sustenance, or because of an assault of a temptation, or because of a devil's attack. Yet such a thing cannot happen to one who listens to the word of God. The soul keeps living because it is consistently nurtured, nor can it fall as a result of a temptation of the flesh or the devil's attack, because it readily finds safety in the divine word as in an impregnable fortress. It is worthwhile, then, that we avail ourselves of this remedy of the divine word. He who makes use of it, it is very true that he will never die.

4. Yet we have to be careful. For the divine word to produce true life in us we have to learn how to take advantage of it. We will do that by guarding it in our heart, on our lips, in our deeds. First of all we have to guard the divine word in our heart by meditating upon it often and especially at the best hour of the day, that is in the morning. We, then, have to love the divine word with affection and think of it often during the day. This makes the pious exercise of a good meditation. We learned from Jesus Christ that he who meditates upon the last things will never sin, never for the eternity, in big or small things.[1]

And since no one can hide such a treasure within his heart without communicating it to others, so that our brothers and sisters may avail themselves of it, so at any occasion we have to speak the divine word with transport of joy, at any event we have to also show in deeds that we are willingly carrying out what the Lord teaches us in his discourses.

What is your reaction to this? I have shown you a remedy to never die, and a very sure remedy indeed. Let all of us avail ourselves of it, and let us do so appropriately.

---

[1] See Sir 7:36

REFLECTIONS

1. A remedy to never die.
2. This remedy is overlooked by the ignorant and the evil ones, while others look for it very eagerly.
3. The divine word makes one live in body and soul.
4. Yet one must cherish it in his heart, profess it with his lips, carry it out in deeds.

GOSPEL OF QUINQUAGESIMA SUNDAY

After laughter weeping is next

1. When you see a madman who has escaped the mental hospital laughing immoderately, you feel a great pity for him, for certainly the unfortunate individual heads for an evil end. As today you see youths who break away from the control of their families, run away from their homes and boldly walk the streets singing and reveling, you, who do not approve it, certainly pity them with all your heart. Those little wretched ones will weep one day, for after laughter weeping follows quickly. The divine Savior, who happened to weep for all his children here below, comes to us today with sadness and says: "As it was written by the prophets... a little while and then the Son of Man will be delivered up to the Gentiles. He will be mocked and outraged and spat upon. They will scourge him and put him to death.... As he drew near Jericho a blind man sat at the side of the road begging... He cried out all the more: 'Lord, I want to see, O Lord that I can see!'"[1] Jesus touched him and the man's eyes were opened.

In doing this act of compassion, Jesus seemed to sigh in his heart: "Oh that all blind sinners could see with the eyes of their mind! These who laugh now in their iniquities would turn their vain joy into a salutary weeping." Very true, my brothers and sisters. This is what the Lord tells us in the book

---

[1] Lk 18: 31-43

of *Proverbs*: "Even in laughter the heart may be sad and the end of joy may be sorrow."[1]

I am going to give you an example. In history we find mentioned Dyonisius, the tyrant of Syracuse. This infamous king was quick in lending himself to all forms of human pleasures. He quickly threw himself into all sorts of ambitions, debaucheries and dishonesties. All the while he could see in the full light of the day the phantoms of the many people he had ruined or damaged. He would run away into the darkness, yet there those furies would scourge him on his flanks. He would get infuriated with everyone and even with himself, yet with more and more anguish. Thinking that he could get rid of them by resorting to the sword, the tyrant gathered around himself assassins and executioners who at his sign would cut off the heads of the members of his court, of people of the city and kingdom. Thus he sent to death the leading people of his state. He threw himself on top of the queen and killed her, then he rushed at his children and crushed them. At this point he felt a fire of hell burning in his stomach. He felt that the entire world was marching against him. He armored himself with an iron breast-plate, let his beard grow long and untidy, and secluded himself in a castle which could be entered only in the evening by a drawbridge. Still he kept seeing ghosts furious for revenge. One desperate night he sat for the last time at a very well furnished table. He ate and then he died in the midst of it. You can ask him now how much good did his pleasures and debaucheries do him!

I hardly believe in these days, improper indeed, that one of you is willing to be led into excesses of great scandal. Yet I cannot hide from you a truth. A pleasure, to do good to

---

[1] Prv 14:13

69

you, must come from the Lord. If it comes from the world it is a poison that sooner or later will make its consequences be felt. There are poisons which show their effects after a month or even a year, while the one who has taken them is not even aware of them and shows no miserable signs. There are other poisons that cause immediate stomach aches.

In regard to human pleasures at times the remorse takes a day or a month, or perhaps a year or two to show up. Yet the longer it takes, the more distressing it will be. Don't envy the merriment of the worldly people a bit! They seem to be happy, but if you could read their hearts!... In the act of merriment they might enjoy themselves, yet wait until the excitement of the wine dies down, reflection creeps in, and the reproaches from the family and the damage for offending God make themselves noticed... Wait and you will see... Better off to renounce the pleasures of the world all together. They are deceitful pleasures.

3. They deceive in this life. And they deceive even more at the hour of death. Think of a drunkard who has spent all his life in squandering his family possessions and now is old, unable to take a step, surrounded by a bleak poverty. Furthermore, imagine that this individual all of a sudden is assaulted by all his creditors who have been patient so far, that the guards are ready to handcuff him, that the executioners are all set to take him up to the podium of death. "Miserable!", everyone would shout to him, "why didn't you learn how to set aside a better bed for your old age? Bear now with what you have set for yourself with so much merriment!"

Yet it will be more cruel for the sinner when he finds out at his death how he took the wrong road, that he had in vain and in sin dissipated the treasure of his years. He will grieve even more in realizing that he has to leave everything behind, like the most unfortunate bankrupt person, leaving even his body as a prey for worms. Then, who will say a word on his behalf at the imminent tribunal of the supreme judge, Jesus Christ? Afer all, it is a matter of an irreversible sentence. It is a matter of being saved in heaven forever, or damned forever in hell. Yet how can one look confidently to heaven when he has laughed at it all the years of his life? So, I don't know what else is left for this dying individual other than the grief sorrow of a very great punishment.

Voltaire, who had busied himself so much in laughing and making others laugh with his vanities and blasphemies, grabbed finally by death, shouted like a possessed man, twisted his body like a snake being crushed underfoot. Not knowing what to hold on, he would grab on his feces, filling his mouth with them out of desperation. Dr. Tronchin, who assisted him, came out with the following remarks: "How horrible is the death of the impious! How dreadful is the death of the impious!" So, laugh if you can! Laugh, but remember that after laughing you will weep, that the best of laughing will be followed by the worst of weeping.

4. Let us all be just and dear to the Lord, so that at least in death we will deserve a much better destiny. Besides we will enjoy it quite a bit even living here on earth.

Consider the days of the just. Privations will be their lot here on earth. The just have to mortify themselves a little. They have to bear with some inconveniences of heat or cold, thirst or hunger, as well as to obey humbly. However, while they are suffering all that, looking up to heaven they can say: "Behold my homeland!" If they look to God they can say: "I love the Lord and hope that he loves me." Listening to the voice of their heart, they seem to hear: "You are for certain saved."

And what a comfort they have in death! Looking at their past, they realize that they have served God and at least they have had a lively desire to please him. Looking at their present, they do not regret leaving their homeland and relatives, because they have already, for quite some time, detached their heart from them. Looking at their future, they feel blessed in seeing paradise waiting for them and in its midst God and all his angels and saints.

Draw now a comparison, my beloved brothers and sisters. Do you think that it is better to laugh now in the midst of evil pleasures or join in the pure joy of virtue? He who has good sense knows what is best for him. If it is better for one to mortify himself here below in order to rejoice in paradise, then begin with renouncing those miserable entertainments pertaining to Carnival which you cannot enjoy without sinning and because of which you are preparing for yourselves the threat of so many evils.

REFLECTIONS

1. After laughter weeping comes next.
2. He who laughs in sin will have to weep in life.
3. He then has to despair in death.
4. Much better it is with the just to renounce evil pleasures.

GOSPEL OF THE FIRST SUNDAY OF LENT

·

Norm for a perfect conversion

1. We have heard about the agony and the death of that ugly figure of paganism, the carnival of worldly people. The fool has disappeared, yet don't think that he is dead. The old man counts already on six thousand years of life, yet remains a foolish bad child. May heaven obtain that this detestable individual may not come back to grab you. Now how do you find yourself? Has this man of sin and blood left in your heart deep scars of sin? Then, repent even more heartily the more you derived enjoyment from the illicit pleasure. The Lord commands you to do that through the words of the prophet Isaiah: "Return, O children of Israel, to him whom you have utterly deserted."[1]

Jesus Christ in today's Gospel presents himself worn out by fasting and tired after overcoming the battle of three temptations waged by Satan. Jesus had been in the desert fasting and praying for forty days when the devil approached him holding two stones and said to him: "Command these stones to turn into bread." Then he suggested to Jesus: "Throw yourself down..., or prostrate yourself in homage to me... I will bestow on you all the kingdoms of the world." Jesus answered: "Not on bread alone is man to live, but on every utterance that comes from the mouth of God... You shall not put the Lord your God to the test... Away with you,

---

[1] Is 31:6

73

Satan!" At that the devil left him, and angels came to wait on him.[1]

Thus God rewards those who fight the enemy from hell. Do you want to overcome the infamous enemy? Then, enter this time of penance. Return to God as eagerly as you had left him before. This is the norm of perfect conversion.

2. The Lord had made magnificent promises to his people Israel by saying to them: "If you love me with all your heart, I will fill you with all blessings from heaven, I will enrich you with all prosperity on earth." He also made to them this threat: "Yet, if you will sadden me with your iniquities, I will punish you with rage." So that, when falling, they would not despair, the Lord said to them through the words of Isaiah we see here: "Return to me whom you have utterly deserted." Most discreet proposal! See how good the Lord is!

Hebrews often lost their patience and murmured gravely against God. Yet, to appease God it was enough for them to stop their sinful behavior and bless the Lord at all times. When the Hebrews in a moment of craziness rushed to adore pagan idols... Not to be cut into pieces or buried alive, it was enough for them to run to the altar of the Most High, fold their hands in prayer and heartily plead: "We have sinned, O Lord. You alone, O God, we all must adore." Thus that people reconciled itself with the Most High and the Most High turned his face with a smile of forgiveness and great pleasure.

The Lord shows even greater tenderness to the Christian people. He embraces these as his dearest children. Foolish, however, would be he who could be filled with the

---

[1] Mt 4:1-11

74

praises from the Lord yet he delays placing himself in his arms!

3. Here, then, you have to distinguish between two kinds of sinners. There are individuals who sin out of frailty of the flesh as David did, or out of frailty of perjury as Peter did. There are, also, other individuals who sin out of malice as Solomon, out of sinful avarice as Judas Iscariot, and after him all the heretics of various times down to the large number who live in our times. In regard to those who sin out of frailty, these sin over a moment and then, repented, quickly return to God. A father considers, as if not existing, an injury which his child has inflicted on him out of a fleeting rage but quickly retracts. Otherwise a malicious offense is deliberate, thereby the sin is qualified. Who has any doubt that such a qualified crime is going to be punished more severely even by civil law?

Thus these wretched individuals, like the repentent Mary Magdalene, must figure out all means for mortifying themsleves so that they may please God. Like repentent Zacchaeus, they must see to it that of what they gathered out of fraud they return to the poor at least fourfold. Like Saul, they must employ zeal in bringing to God the greatest possible number of just souls, in order to make up for the many they have brought to ruin because of their scandals.

Furthermore isn't it proper for you to strive to serve the Lord with equal care as you strived to offend him before?

4. There are, also, sinners who degrade themselves down to the bottom of iniquity. These commit all sorts of wickednesses and then they make scorn of them. These individuals imitate the leaders of the Hebrew people or the mockeries instigated by them against the adorable person of

the Savior. The more they knew those injuries would cause torment to the Lord, the more those individuals made fun of the whole ordeal. When, finally, they saw Jesus hanging on the cross, they came around to ridicule him more gaily. It is difficult for these individuals to repent in their heart.

However, if it happened that Longinus stroke his chest, it is expected that one who in his past never said, "This is it with doing evil!", now determines not to stop performing good deeds. This individual should pray, adding to it a frequent reception of the Sacraments, as well as giving alms and performing works of piety, punishing his body and concluding: "I am a useless servant, O Lord. Have mercy on me, you whose mercy is infinite". Likewise Taide, after repenting from being a public sinner, turned her gaze to heaven and prayed: "You who have created me, have mercy on me!" Taide didn't even dare using the holy name of the Lord, considering herself worthy only of punishing her tongue with dust and adding bruises to the beatings she inflicted upon her sinful body.

5. Furthermore there are sinners who have turned their heart from the softness of the flesh to the hardness of the stone. There are other sinners who have taken the eyes out of their mind in order not to believe. Still others who, like Pharaoh, said: "Who is the Lord of heaven whom should I obey?", or like the foolish Nabuchonezzar who had a statue erected in his resemblance and demanded: "All of you adore me, for there is no god greater than the golden statue I am giving you."

Such is the scandal unheard of which our eyes have seen in these days when, carrying the flag of Satan in parade, people have cried out in full daylight in center city: "Long live Satan! Long live hell!" We don't know whether a worse scandal has ever been seen on the face of the earth. This outrageous impiety made all believers shudder.

If ever one of these individuals repents, it is better for him that he does not do only as we suggested above, but he treads upon every consideration for himself. It is good that he walks openly in the city streets wearing the sackcloth of the penitent, crying out loudly: "Mercy!" More than anyone else this individual has scandalized souls. It is appropriate, then, that more than anyone else he sees to it that he makes up for his evil example. Don't think that what he is expected to do is something over and above: it is just of mere justice. Better off for him if he gets as close to the Lord now as he had moved far away from him before.

6. It may look strange to see how Israel, that means a child who is dear to the Lord, down the road has become so wicked. Do you believe that Judas was not at least good enough when he was welcomed into the following of the divine Savior? The unlucky man became evil when, after being entrusted with the group's purse, he tried excessively to steal from it, increase it, attaching his heart to it too inordinately.

Useless to say how easy it is to fall off little by little from plenty of good into an abyss of evil. Much more, in going down it is easier that one tumbles rather than paces down. A small flake of snow, after separating from the top of the mountain, rolls down and little by little turns into an avalanche that rushes down, crushing trees and houses in its way. How much should we fear the little faults, when they are deliberate! Taking a step backword at the point when one is going to reach the top of the mountain of perfection could be enough to bring him to ruin down a mortal steep descent.

7. Finally, if someone little by little or suddenly tumbled down, if he wants to stand up he has to do it not little by little but quickly and with determination. Let him invoke with his heart for God's grace, because God, who promised it, will give it to him with no doubt. With the assistance of this grace he will be able not only to run, but even fly, as Pelagia, Taide, Theodore, and William Aquitanus did.

It is necessary that we entrust ourselves to God and hasten, because proceding at the usual pace one could run the risk that, because of the weight of his evil habit, he might take one step forward and three backward. Here is given to you, as briefly and clearly as possible, the norm of a perfect contrition. We are all sinners, in big or small things: we all need to keep before our memory this rule of conversion so that we may heartily go back to the holy love of the Lord.

REFLECTIONS

1. A norm for a perfect conversion.
2. God wants that a sinner gets as close to him now, as he was far from him when he ran away from him.
3. He who sins out of frailty can quickly return to God. He who sins out of malice must make use of many means to please God.
4. Much more so if, in sinning, he made fun of God.
5. Worse still, if he boasted of sinning.
6. Little by little, even a faithful Christian may fall into an excessive fault.
7. To come out of it, he must not just walk, but hasten with wings in his feet.

GOSPEL OF THE SECOND SUNDAY OF LENT

A fortunate reward

1. There may be found many among worldly people who, in order to achieve a place of honor or gain, spend a lot of time, enduring incredible privations due to hunger, thirst, tribulations and dangers. They are lucky, then, if after laboring so much they are able to obtain the favor of a powerful individual, or step into a hall, or gain employment at high places. The majority of them, nonetheless, do not attain those positions or when they do, it is late.

More fortunate are the followers of the divine Savior. These experience great consolations in their spirit for the labors they sustain for God, and then they find the gates of heaven wide open before themselves. An angel of the Lord comes to say to them: "Behold the wages for your suffering, come faithful of the Lord!"

"You are the ones who have endured with me my trials and I," Jesus Christ says, "will give you the kingdom that my Father prepared for me, so that you may eat and drink at my table, in my kingdom."[1] In today's Gospel we read that the divine Savior, speaking to Peter, James and John, said: "It has been a while now that you have endured sufferings with me, now come for I want to show you a thing of great consolation." He led them up on Mt. Tabor and there he was transfigured before their eyes. The face of Jesus became as dazzling as the sun, his clothes as radiant as light. In fixing

---

[1] Lk 22:28-30

their eyes on such a beauty, the apostles seemed to be never tired and were already proposing to remain there forever. Yet Jesus said to them: "The time to enjoy has not come yet; what I have shown you is only a sample of what I have prepared for you and will be granted to you in my paradise."[1]

So, let us console ourselves, my brothers and sisters. If we have to bear with some kind of pain, God will reward us for it. "So great is the reward that awaits me that every pain is a pleasure for me", sings the soul that longs for paradise. Let us long for it ourselves, for certainly the heavenly kingdom is a blessed reward. That kingdom will be granted to us after we have endured with constancy till the end.

2. Long for paradise! Long for paradise! There is a kingdom that holds a banquet without end. Tribulation and sorrow are felt no more there. What a pleasure to be part of such a banquet! This is the banquet in the kingdom of our heavenly Father. It is called banquet not because the blessed do nothing but eat or drink there. As a matter of fact, the blessed do not eat or drink for the eternity, for they have no need for it.

Jesus spoke in these terms to his disciples because they were uncouth and hardly able to understand spiritual matters. Jesus said to them: "At a pleasant banquet one satisfies his appetite, pleasing his eyes with its sight and his palate with its taste. As his whole body is filled with enjoyment, so in the kingdom of my heavenly Father man's appetite will be fully satisfied." His eyes will be happy to see God, his ears rejoice in hearing angelic melodies, his touch in feeling the presence of the beatific vision. Furthermore man's faculties of his intellect, memory and will will also be satisfied since they

---

[1] See Mt 17:1-9

will find in God the source of every beatitude. My brothers and sisters, then, don't you think that we should long for this heavenly banquet more than anything else?

3. There will be closer to God at his banquet those who have followed Jesus Christ closer here on earth. The apostles followed him first and more valiantly, so these are the ones whom the divine Savior claims to be with him at his banquet. Later on he adds that each of them will sit on a throne similar to his own to judge the tribes of Israel. Worthy apostles of the Lord, you who are the princes in the heavenly court, intercede for us and assist us. Be benevolent toward us when you will come with Jesus to judge the earth. We, on our part, let us keep up with courage in following our divine Savior. The more faithful we will be in enduring our trials, the closer the Lord will have us sit at his table in paradise.

King Ahasuerus gave a great feast of seven days in the garden court of the royal palace for all the people, great and small, who were in the stronghold of Susa. The king ordered that the greatest of his kingdom sat right close to him, while the others would be at their seats all the way down by degrees, with enjoyment and merriment for everyone.

What pleasure will be ours when we will be at the table in paradise, along with all those who were saved until the end of the world? I cannot describe it from down here on earth, since the joy we talk about is a pleasure that belongs to heaven.

4. However, I know very well that such a bliss will be ours if we follow Christ; it will be ours as it has been given to the apostles.

Take a closer look at these heroes. They joined Jesus Christ. To follow him, they gave up everything on earth. They even gave up their homeland and relatives. Furthermore they followed Jesus faithfully, sleeping on the floor at night as he did, suffering hunger or begging and being reproached and openly persecuted during the day. They followed Jesus also in the most difficult circumstances when he was slandered as a blasphemer or an insurrectionist. When they put their hands on him to kill him, the apostles did not run away but stayed there with constancy.

For all this Jesus Christ has given them the kingdom which the eternal Father had given to Jesus himself. There is one difference only: Jesus received the kingdom by nature, the apostles by grace. Otherwise the kingdom is the same: through love, in its greatness and in the substance of its blessedness.

We, little wretched ones, can gain that kingdom as the apostles did! As a matter of fact, Jesus Christ intercedes and sees to it that it may be granted to us with certainty. There is one sole condition: to suffer for God here on earth so that we may be in his company in glory. How foolish we would be if, being able to sit with God at his blessed banquet, we neglected to merit immediately a beautiful place of honor!

5. You might object that even the apostles abandoned their divine master, though only for a little while. That's true that they abandoned him briefly, and you know that when the separation is only momentarily, is not even considered as such. Besides, when Jesus said: "You will sit with me at the banquet in my kingdom", this kind of unfaithfulness had not taken place yet. This separation resembles the straying of sheep on the occasion of a storm when the thunder resounds in the mountains, the flashes blind one's sight and the lightnings strike down. Once the storm is over, the sheep hear

the voice of their shepherd again and run to meet him to graze from his hand as if to thank him for saving them.

Be comforted, then, my brothers and sisters. If, however, and may heaven spare you, you fell in the storm of a temptation, rise immediately, if you want that God embrace you. Unfortunately there are Christians who, after going to confession, fall again into a grave sin and dwell in it for weeks or even months. These prove that they care little for the grace and the reward of God. Oh that individuals like these may not be in our midst! To be able to sit at the banquet with Jesus in the heavenly kingdom is a reward which we must secure for ourselves with all the strengths of our soul.

REFLECTIONS

1. A blessed reward.
2. This is the banquet in the kingdom in paradise.
3. The more one has suffered for Christ, the more he will enjoy in that blessed kingdom.
4. The apostles were the first and most valiant ones in following Jesus.
5. If they left him for a moment on the occasion of a storm, they certainly went back to him hastily afterwards.

GOSPEL OF THE THIRD SUNDAY
OF LENT

Behold the Lord!

1. There are pious souls who find themselves in the midst of some kind of tribulation and anxiously question: "Where is the Lord?" Just souls, why do you fear? Behold the Lord! He is in your midst. There are sinful souls who complain saying: "Where is the Lord?..." You have driven him out of the site of your heart, yet he surrounds you to see whether you let him enter through the door of your heart. He makes himself heard with a loving voice. Behold the Lord! He awaits to embrace you.

Today's Gospel presents to us the figure of a miserable sinner, possessed by the devil, deaf and mute. Most unfortunate, he cried out for help. Jesus Christ heard him, came to him and cast Satan out of that man. Then he opened the ears of the wretched man and freed his tongue. Yet, would you believe it? The crowds who witnessed this double miracle of grace, began to murmur: "It is by Beelzebub, the prince of devils, that he casts out Satan."[1]

How blind! That's horrible! That's horrible! The Savior is in their midst and they are not even aware of it. Are we, on our part, more aware of it? Let us open the eyes of our faith. Let us all take a closer look. Behold the Lord who shows himself to us, why do we delay in entrusting ourselves to him with all our heart?

---

[1] Lk 11: 14-28

2. Look at the little lamb that frisks about in the field and then bleats calling for his mother: that is a dear little animal, but try to tell him to stop bleating. His mother is there and follows each step of her little lamb. Lambs of the Lord, good followers of Jesus Christ, you enjoy being in the field of Christian piety and with contentment you go through the field of good deeds. May God bless you. Yet what about your continuous questioning: "Where is my Lord?" All along you bother the confessors and annoy friends and relatives as well. Be quiet, for God's sake. Don't you see that the Lord is in your midst?

You might say that you do not hear him, that you do not see him. Is God, perhaps, material so as to be seen with your eyes or heard with your ears or felt with your heart? Many times he manages to be sensed this way, because of that admirable connection that exists between one's body and his spirit.

However, if he does not do so quickly, why do you get so upset about it? Is it not good enough that God dwells in your heart, even though he does not make himself felt sensibly! Behold the Lord! Be quiet! The Lord is with you!

3. Others beside you need to worry about it. It is those who do not understand anything about God or even do not care for him at all, who need to worry. These are more guilty, indeed. In some way they share in the malice that belonged to the Hebrews.

Jesus Christ was in their midst in Judea and manifested his presence by his heavenly preaching, by supernatural miracles. Still, the crowd did not understand him or did not care for what they had understood. When Jesus cast out a demon and healed the man who was also deaf and mute, the crowd cried out: "This man casts out devils by the power of the prince of the devils!" Thus that crowd became like a beast, so much so that the divine Savior himself finally had to curse them saying: "Woe to you for driving me out of your city so shamefully!... You and your children will bear the punishment for shedding my blood..." It is two thousand years that this terrible curse weights horribly on the heads of the killers of God.

Let's come to ourselves. There is no doubt that God makes the power of his voice and the industries of his pious love felt in our heart. Yet, how do we listen to him? How slow we are in our mind in knowing the ways of the Lord! How slow we are in our heart in practicing the suggestions of the divine inspirations! Truly we need that God restore the hearing in our ears, that the Lord open the door of our heart!

4. Let us give our cooperation and let us avail ourselves in it of the wings of faith. Let us make use of the support of our imagination. Here I give you an example.

Suppose your house becomes the house of the king and that he comes to reside in it. Who does not know that where a king lives, he is seen as he is, in all his individuality? From his room he is present in all parts of his kingdom, since he knows what it is there, runs everything that needs to be done, and cares for it with magnificent bounty.

That is the way God lives in the heart of the just. He lives in it more than the king in that house, because while the king is in one room he cannot be physically present in another nor equally in any other place outside of it. Instead God is present totally to all the senses of our body, present to all the faculties of our spirit. He is present to each individual in the world and to all human beings in general, because God is the almighty.

What do you think? Let us revere God, then, with all the acts of the mind and give homage with the affections of the heart, without giving him displeasure of any sort. What would you say of one who, having been granted a visit by the king, shows more than one act of incivility, slight as it might be, against him?... And we, reflecting that God is present in our heart, should beware of committing any sort of sin both grave or venial.

5. Rather, we should hold on to him with all the affections of our heart. When the illustrious majesty of a bishop or of a pope enters our house we do everything to keep him proper company. Think of the enthusiasm which good Catholics showed in receiving in their cities and houses the much vexed popes like Pius VI and Pius VII. They did not stop from kneeling before them, asking for their holy blessing, applauding with great joy and wishing prosperity to the Vicar of the divine Savior.

Well, he who dwells in the house of our heart is not just an individual of this earth, though lofty in dignity. It is God who dwells in it, the glory of paradise, Jesus Christ, who is our salvation. Thus you will learn how to answer back those ungrateful and ill-mannered individuals who say: "It is enough to say hello to the Lord once on feast days or think of him at the time of death." Most ungrateful individuals! The angels in heaven never stop singing to God: "Alleluia, alleluia!" We should do more, because we are the creatures benefited by the Lord more than they, and besides we need his assistance. As a consequence, we should do nothing but give praises to him at all the hours of the day. We should do nothing but say: "Blessed be, Lord, our God, forever and praised by all!", and so keep up with expressing to him our consistent affections of faith, humility, thanksgiving, as they can only please the majesty of the Most High. Then the regret that makes you say, "Where is God?", will vanish from you. And also will vanish the disturbance that you cause to others who must remind you at all times: "Behold the Lord!"

REFLECTIONS

1. Behold the Lord!
2. He is in the heart of the just.
3. He is with the sinners to embrace them if they welcome him.
4. Behold the Lord!
5. Let us all adhore him.

GOSPEL OF THE FOURTH SUNDAY OF LENT

Apostolic lifestyle

1. Jesus Christ has come to teach us how to live here on earth. We read in the holy Gospel that, when Jesus preached, crowds gathered around him to listen to him. It also happened that they followed him to the top of a mountain, happy to hang on to his lips, ready even to suffer hunger and deprivation. They had been following him for three days now, in the solitude of the desert. Jesus felt pity for them and when five loaves of bread and a couple of dried fishes were brought to him, he blessed them and had them distributed to the crowd. They all had their fill. After gathering the leftovers they filled twelve baskets. The crowd raised their hands and voices to praise the providence of Jesus the savior. With five loaves of bread and a couple of dried fish the divine Savior satisfies the crowds.[1]

Here we have, as far as our bodily life goes, the rule which the divine Savior brought down to earth from heaven. A bit of bread and a few fish, that is just what is strictly necessary to live. This custom which Jesus applied to himself, and recommended to others, became a custom for the apostolic life. For all St. Paul wrote to Timothy: "If we have food and clothing we have all that we need. Those who want to be rich are falling into temptation and a trap. They are letting themselves be captured by foolish and harmful desires

---

[1] See Jn 6: 1-15

which drag men down to ruin and destruction."[1] On the substance of this discourse is briefly based the standard of living of apostolic life and at the same time the dangers of a worldly and epicurean life are pointed out. Let us examine the safety of the one as well as the dangers of the other and let us learn from them.

2. It is very true that man becomes accustomed, in a special way in his younger age, to certain foods, clothing, and living quarters, to which, as shabby as they might be, he intends to adjust according to his needs. Man lives in any climate, warm or cold, dry or humid. Our body adjusts to any kind of treatment. Yet it has the property that, if you begin with treating it roughly, it will become tamed like a horse so as to be content with a little straw and a miserable shelter in a cave or a hut. But if you begin with caressing it, the soft body becomes demanding and even arrogant, and finally a cruel tyrant.

So, what do you think now? Didn't the Apostle benefit us greatly by pointing out to us that once our body has enough to eat and be clothed with, we should be content with that? A man should look for not more than a piece of bread, a set of clothing, and a house. If he does so he is fortunate, because with a moderate wage he can happily care for the slave of his body.

Make a simple observation here. Are not the people dwelling in the mountains, who actually live according to the apostolic and patriarchal way, happier and more healthy and prosperous than those who live in the city and the plains, engulfed with all the pleasures of an effeminate softness?...

---

[1] 1 Tm 6:8-9

3. When you see people who are overly anxious in securing earthly riches, you should be greatly horrified. Those wretched ones, by immoderately seeking wealth, they seek the devil money, which is the most terrible among all devils. This demon lays snares everywhere and lures people to fall into them. Once they are caught, he sets a string around their necks, holding them tight so that they cannot be free any more. How difficult it is that at least one among the many gets free! Especially when the riches have been gained through frauds and cheats, it is barely possible that one gets rid of them by quieting down the cries of the deceived widow or of the betrayed orphan.

What happens then? Those who immoderately seek after riches, become involved with multiple preoccupations. Worrying about so many earthly matters, how can they think about securing for themselves the highest interest of eternal salvation, for which all the thoughts and cares of one's life are never enough?

Actually the traffickers of earthly things get involved with most vain preoccupations. To procure for themselves every comfort of life, every liesure in the house, every occasion for pleasure, is the greatest care of the men of pleasure. Worst still, for they indulge themselves with obscenities openly, as well as with excesses and scandals. From these they derive ailments in their body and even death. But most of all from them they gain perdition, that is the ruin of their soul. Once the soul is lost, it is lost for good. It is not regained through tears of blood, nor is it redeemed through the sacrifice of suffering. Ponder seriously upon this standard of merrymaking life that leads to such a terrible end. Consider the good fruits of apostolic lifestyle and all along avail yourselves of it as a norm for your lifestyle.

4. Don't keep coming back to tell me that one can very well seek even riches and improve his social status without running any risk of damnation. Do not say that, for the Apostle is very clear about it. He says that those who inordinantly seek after riches *incidunt*, that is, fall automatically into temptation, into the trap set by Satan. One who attaches himself immoderately to riches, immediately stops thinking of his soul in a serious manner, immediately stops loving God above all, and instantly falls into the snares we have mentioned above.

If you want to be impartial in judging yourselves or the neighbor whom you have noticed craving for earthly riches, you will find out that both you and your neighbors have set aside the business of the salvation of your soul.

In a special way the farmers who leave behind farming in order to get involved with the noise of city businesses, these are the first ones who allow themselves to be lured by the craziness of pleasures, and the first ones to be ruined. They are followed by more and more people who, although being able to live where they are according to their needs, leave their families and their homeland to seek overseas a life according to their pleasure, a fortune that is very costly. Even among these, how many illusioned and deceived are there who at the end get lost! We pray to the Lord that he may keep his holy hands on our heads. To seek riches and then be damned is a matter of a moment.

REFLECTIONS

1. Apostolic lifestyle.
2. A characteristic of apostolic lifestyle is to live according to basic needs.
3. A characteristic of the merrymaking lifestyle is to live for pleasures.
4. It is not possible to live for pleasures and then save one's soul.

GOSPEL OF PASSION SUNDAY

An annoying friend

1. In society you find certain friends who are so
annoying that you wonder whether you were better off
without them. They are suspicious and untrustworthy. They
are quick in criticizing every step you take and every word
you say. They are very forward in asking you for things, yet
very poor in responding with assistance to or affection for
you. Often they may directly or indirectly plot tricks and by
abusing the title of being your friends they cause the worst
evil that ruthless adversaries could think of.

Such seemed to be the Hebrews mentioned in today's
Gospel. They had Jesus in their midst who was showering
them with every blessing and pointing out to them a teaching
from heaven. Yet those miserable ones did not care for it.
They rather turned to criticize his discourses and deeds. In
today's Gospel while Jesus says, "Whoever is of God hears
every word that God speaks", the Jews retorted with
harshness: "Now we are sure you are possessed". The divine
Savior explained himself, yet the audience did not want to
hear. Finally, to silence him, they picked up rocks to throw at
him.[1]

Most annoying friends, you, Hebrews, have become; a
nation that had been dear to the Lord. Yet, are not certain
lukewarm and almost indifferent Christians today any less
annoying? May heaven spare you from belonging to this
category of friends who are so inconsiderate and annoying

---

[1] Jn 8 : 46-59

that just thinking of them makes one get angry. Let us see and find out, for this is very important indeed.

In the *Book of Revelation* written by St. John we read that the Lord speaks so terribly as follows: "I know your deeds; I know you are neither hot nor cold. How I wish you were one or the other - hot or cold! But because you are lukewarm, neither hot nor cold, I will spew you out of my mouth!" [1] How do you feel in hearing this? I am horrified. Let us see how appropriate it is for us to fear about this.

2. Let us reflect on two possibilities which are quite common and not at all unusual. You go to visit an individual whom you consider a friend, a relative of yours, whose character you do not know in depth, however. This person is quite kind to you and you leave rather satisfied. You say to yourself: "It is not a small thing that he has shown me kindness at my first visit. He surely will be more benevolent to me next time." Now, pay attention to this. Sinners, you have been away from the Lord in the past. Though not that enthused toward him, if you begin to visit him and offer him in homage the affections of your heart, certainly he will not reject you. Actually you are lukewarm friends, yet you show that you intend to become more fervent in the future.

Or you have come to visit a friend who has been very courteous in showing you all the comforts of his house and of his personal care for you in the past, yet now he seems to be rather cold in your regard. He greets you coldly, and carelessly asks you to sit awhile, acting as if to say that he is already tired of you. How hurt would you be! How disappointed! You can't believe it, and with a heavy heart you say to yourself:

---

[1] Rv 3: !5-16

"Let me get out of here, out of here quickly! How annoying this friend has become to me, who used to be so dear!"

Draw out yourself the application now. Have you been so far fervent in the service of the Lord and solicitous for God?... Now you find yourself regressed, your heart withered in its affection, your mind bored in thinking of God, and so you neglect saying your prayers, receiving the Sacraments, doing works of mercy... Alas! Alas! Be frightened, before the Lord may say to you: "*Incipiam te evomere ex ore meo.* I am beginning to spew you out of my mouth. I am getting to feel a loathing for you, as you have shown to feel a loathing for me."

3. What is happening now? ... A total breaking off of relations with God, a declared hostility that becomes even more dismal. What happened to you after your lukewarm friend, mentioned above, showed himself to be so bored with you?... You stopped visiting him and he avoided meeting you, so all the affection of the past has turned into a most fierce hatred.

When a boiling caldron is removed from the firing coals it loses its heat and little by little becomes deadly cold. My Christian brothers and sisters, after being filled with fervor at the furnace of Jesus' love in the most holy Sacrament, woe to us if we end up by becoming cold! We would be better off if we were never warm! We would be better off if we never knew Jesus Christ, rather than abandoning him so wickedly after having known him!

4. If you like, we could compare our heart to that mysterious chariot which appeared to the army of Judas Maccabee to spur them on to fight and helped them to defeat their enemies. Our heart is like a chariot pulled by horses, if

you wish, which are fiery and eager to race. They paw the ground to lead forward, yet it is impossible for them to know how to back up or follow.

Once our heart has learned how to love God, it runs fast toward paradise and never tires with expatiating in those endless regions. But when the heart stops, or cools down, it dies. It does not move anymore. Miserable heart! Better off if it never moved!

Saul lasted for a long while in his glacial coldness, yet when he woke up he became Paul, that is a chosen vessel and an apostle of great preaching. A miracle of grace is needed so that one who has fallen from fervor into lukewarmness may revive. St. Teresa had reached that miserable point. She had abandoned her pious meditations, her most devout devotions and had turned to vain readings and dangerous fashions. God, then, appeared to her and opening hell wide before her eyes, said: "Behold your dwelling! If you do not wake up, you will be lost forever". She was a lucky daughter, for she was frightened on time and repented.

What about us?... If we realize that we are lukewarm, let us not wait until God decides to work out such a miracle, because God rarely works that way. Let us wake up before lukewarmness takes us to become frozen.

5. Do you want to learn about the symptoms of this fatal lukewarmness? The first one is a weakening of faith, a darkening of the intellect and a beginning boredom in the good practices of piety and religion. At this point God has not abandoned you yet, but decreases his favors and cuts down in the abundance of his grace.

The second sign of lukewarmness is our neglect of practices of piety, of pious meditations, of our imploring prayers, of letting our neighbor walk the wrong path and not being bothered by it. All these are symptoms that a Christian is abandoning God and is becoming engulfed with earthly pleasures.

Finally there comes the hardening of the heart, and the blinding of the intellect, which are clear signs not just of lukewarmness but of cold death.

6. Reflect on the evilness of this sin: declaring oneself of being a friend and then detaching oneself from it little by little. Knowing God and then turning to the devil of vanity and pride. From almost touching paradise and then backing away from it in order to get engulfed into a putrid swamp, one can say whatever he wants, still it is a very wicked iniquity, an ungratefulness that upsets one's stomach. So, you can understand the deep annoyance caused by a lukewarm friend. May heaven spare you from being lukewarm Christians.

REFLECTIONS

1. An annoying friend.
2. Two cases of a lukewarm friend.
3. He who slackens from being a fervent friend will end up becoming a declared enemy.
4. To go back to the original friendship takes a miracle.
5. Signs of lukewarmness.
6. He who leaves God for the earth is a stomach-upsetting Christian.

GOSPEL OF PALM SUNDAY

A faithful servant

1. Let us all be faithful servants of our Lord. The history of humankind is too regrettable to be remembered. How many people have failed being faithful to God! How many do fail today! Today's Gospel recounts how the Hebrews crowded to meet Jesus entering the city of Jerusalem in triumph. Even the children, carrying olive branches in their hands, exclaimed: "Hosanna to the Son of David! Blessed is he who comes in the name of the Lord." [1]

Jesus, however, instead of feeling good about it, was saddened and tears flowed from his eyes, for he knew very well that on the following days that same crowd would cry out loudly and with great indignation: "Crucify him! Crucify him!"

Brothers and sisters, how great our misery is! Let us be confounded by it. This morning many of us have applauded in receiving the holy Sacraments. We have said: "Hosanna to the Son of David. Blessed is he who has come in the name of the Lord". Others are getting ready to express the same greeting of jubilation and I congratulate them all. However, let us nail down a resolution today. Let us be faithful servants of the Lord not only for a day or a few months, let us be so forever. St. John in his *Book of Revelation* warns us in the name of God: "Remain faithful until death and I will give you the crown of life."[2]

---

[1] See Mt 21: 1-9
[2] Rv 2: 10

2. Let us be, then, servants faithful to God. To be a faithful servant means to have a good heart in handling the interests of the master even better than one's own.

When two individuals are friends it means they consider one another equal in esteem and status. To be faithful it is enough that a friend handles the interests of his friend with the same care he handles his own. A master is much more than his servant. So, when a prince takes someone from the populace to work in his royal palace, he expects him to care for the interests of his master, which are of great importance, much more than for his own, which are of very little account. Better off that the clogs of the servant catch on fire than the noble clothing of the prince! On this condition one is considered being a faithful servant and thereby is given a copious wage.

Let us apply this similarity to our case. We are the servants and the Most High is our lord. How much better it is that our goods disappear than God's glory, our health rather than God's honor, our very life than the adorable person of the Savior! Do we believe that we are willing to give up everything rather than to lose the divine grace? Let us keep in mind that only on this condition we will be able to believe that we are faithful servants, and then we will be able to receive from God a crown of merit.

3. For now I will tell you what it means to claim to be faithful servants until death. It means that, if the emaciated figure of misery comes about and lasts as the famine in Egypt and even more, until the end of our lives, we should submit to it for good. It means that if the stench and torment of an illness afflicts us, as Job laying on his heap of manure, for a long time, we should consistently look to God and pray to him to grant us virtue and never lose patience. It means that if

the horror of a calumny weighed on us as on the chaste Susana, or that the pain of internal aridity afflicted our heart, as the heart of Jesus was tormented in the garden of Gethsemani, even then we should say: "If this chalice cannot pass by without me drinking it, *fiat voluntas tua* - your will be done"[1], and persevere in doing good. This is what it means to be servants faithful to God until death. Isn't it much better to bear with some kind of torment in life and then receive the crown of triumph in death?

4. Are you scared by the thought that death will delay a hundred years before she takes you? Do not be afraid, for it will not take long. Death will come much sooner. Who can assure you that death is not in town and even entering the threshold of your house? If she finds you busy waiting for her, blessed are you! If she finds you distracted by thousands of other preoccupations, miserable you are forever! Patience, then, my brothers and sisters, is needed. It will be only for a brief period of time. Death will come even sooner than you would think, and if she finds you in the act of faithful servants, she will crown you with the crown of life.

5. Most dear crown! It is said here on earth that one has obtained the crown of a long, rich, prosperous life, the crown of a glorious and illustrious life, when he has enjoyed the best of what one can ever desire in a long-lived, healthy life, filled with riches, glorious for its abundance in knowledge, illustrious for its achievement in matters of art or discoveries.

In paradise there will be the true crown of life, since life from a passing one will turn to be eternal. Besides, there, life becomes tranquil, fully prosperous, glorious, since the life

---

[1] See Lk 22: 42

that is enjoyed there is the very life of God. Most dear crown of life, how much do I long for you! What is one's forbearance here below, when the crown of life that awaits us is so perfect in beauty and enjoyment?

6. Furthermore, do not fear that God may not give you such a crown. He has to give it to us. He has promised us so. It is out of justice that he gives it to us. Did you ever hear that a magnificent king denied the wage to his servant who earned it? Would you ever think that God may deny the crown of life to his faithful servants? Ahasuerus heartily set the crown on Mordecai's head when he recognized the intimate faithfulness of his good servant. The Lord is much richer, much better and much more just. Let us have no doubt about it. He will give us a crown much richer than we can even imagine. Let us do what we are expected to do on our part. Let us remain servants faithful until the end and God will grant us the crown of life.

REFLECTIONS

1. Faithful servant.
2. As faithful servants let us handle God's interests better than our own.
3. Let us endure in this faithfulness at all cost until death.
4. Death will not delay.
5. Then God will grant us the crown of life.
6. He is obliged to do so and he will give it to us with immense love.

GOSPEL OF THE SUNDAY
IN ALBIS

Homeland, homeland!

1. Jesus, our captain and father, has left the darkness of the tomb. He raised from death and he is now glorious and immortal. Jesus Christ in his glorified body goes through closed windows and locked doors. With his spirit that is the love of God he announces the lot of all good to men. He greets his disciples and his faithful followers, saying: "May God's peace be with you". Then, breathing on them his breath of divine power, he gives them the power to bring souls back to life, as one day with his divine breath he drew a human body from a mass of clay. He says to his disciples: "Receive the Holy Spirit; if you forgive men's sins, they are forgiven them; if you hold them bound, they are held bound". To make them realize that it was not a ghost speaking to them, he asked them, "Probe with your hands the nailprints in my hands and in my feet, for I am, Jesus your savior."[1]

Through these admirable events of divine power and dear discourses of divine mercy, Jesus Christ seems to say: "My disciples, what are you still thinking of or looking at? Homeland, homeland!" The apostles of the divine Savior took good advantage of this. Looking to paradise ecstatically as everyone else, Peter wrote to the faithful all over the world: "Beloved, you are strangers and in exile; hence I urge you not to indulge your carnal desires. By their nature they wage war on the soul. Conduct yourselves blamelessly among the

---

[1] See Jn 20: 19-31

pagans."[1] What do we do now? Let us listen to the apostle. Let us journey as pilgrims here on earth and let us cry out all along: "Homeland, homeland!"

2. Imagine that three individuals come to knock at the door of your house at different times. A character of a fellow comes and happily says to you that it is the first day of carnival, so: "Let us not delay in merrymaking!" This rascal makes you mad, isn't it true? So, let him go, for he is an earthly citizen. He thinks he is going to be eternal here on earth and never leave it. Leave him alone, for he is a bad Christian.

A way-farer, all covered with dust because of his long journey, comes by and asks to be your guest so that he may enjoy a joyful evening with you and then take his rest in a comfortable bed. You know him and welcome him. He is a guest and deserves not to be rejected. He is the image of those Christians who live as foreigners here on earth, because they know well that they are not going to dwell here below forever. They see paradise and long for it, yet while they are living on earth they do not want to miss any pleasure they can get from it. Deceived Christians! You are not evil, no, yet how much better you could be! You acknowledge the fact that you are pilgrims here; why, then, don't you live as pilgrims?

Behold the third figure that comes to your door. He is a pilgrim. He comes to you wearing no hat, barefoot, carrying one bag over his shoulders. He looks pitiful in his garments. You are touched by it and offer him the best you can afford in your house. The fortunate man, however, says to you: "I am a way-farer, a piece of bread is enough for me. Tomorrow morning, at dawn, I will depart to see my homeland. Any

---

[1] 1 Pt 2: 11f.

corner in the house is enough for my brief rest." And he intones right away: "Homeland! Homeland!", and in singing his face becomes radiant with joy. In listening to him you cry out of tenderness. You join in with the singing of that pitiful man and repeat: "Homeland! Homeland!"

This is the story of humankind here on earth. Here you have an image of Christendom. There are people who live like merrymakers: these are the evil ones. There are people who live like foreigners. These are the ordinary Christians. There are others who live like way-farers: these are the perfect Christians. To which category does each of us belong?

3. He who is an evil Christian, please, leave, for this talk is not for you. Here in this place we are glad to speak to those who live as pilgrims or at least as foreigners. So, you who are good, renounce the cravings of the flesh. Does a pleasure of the flesh benefit you a bit? Does a little bit of pride in your mind make you a little bigger, or the profit of material goods add to your happiness? Don't bother with it not even a little bit! What are you doing?

Above all, do not give in by desiring the pleasures of the flesh. The flesh is too big a lier. If you please it with a simple thought of lust, it immediately asks for an act of it, thereby turning you into earthly Christians, that is disabled, fickle, blind and most contrary to thinking about your future to come. Pay attention to me. Don't give any satisfaction to the expectations of the flesh. Have you not already found out that the fire of the flesh is caused by a spark as in a pile of straw or pieces of wood well staked? Let us all think of our homeland, and never for a moment think of corporal pleasures.

4. Very true, those ill-omened thoughts become dearing in entering our house and sit at our table, as flies bother us at our desks, as the swallows annoy us under the gutters of our houses. Well, it is enough that you do not spread honey around for the flies to gather in swarms, it is enough not to ask the swallows to nest close to our bedroom. As a matter of fact, the flies leave quickly when you set a trap for them with acid water or purposely setting your rooms in the dark. The swallows, when they disturb too much, are quickly led to leave by closing the opening to their nests. Likewise you should do with your troublesome thoughts. Let us get rid of them immediately. Let us turn our attention to something else. When evil thoughts bother us, let us not even stare at them. In looking at them, they act like the asp, who, if it succeeds in fixing its look penetrating into our eyes, makes us dizzy and then poisons us. We have to flee away from evil thoughts. The devils flee in confusion when they find themselves abandoned.

5. The following must also be observed. We have to live here on earth, that is in the midst of a society of all kinds of people. There are people who are Christians only by name, but actually they are pagans. What can we do in the midst of such great confusion of people?

You need to be very cautious. You have to walk on the top of dragons and serpents without being wounded. You need attention and courage. I would say that you need faith and prayer. When we speak to people, let us make use of words and answer the questions, all the while keeping our eyes directed to God, our heart longing for paradise, our mind concentrated on the last things to come. Let us guard ourselves from a word, or a sneer that might in someway feed in with a thought less than honest.

This is the way to live as a pilgrim here below. We must not attach ourselves to people or the pleasures of the earth, but turning our eyes to heaven we should exclaim: "Homeland! Homeland!", and strive for paradise with all our strengths.

REFLECTIONS

1. Homeland! Homeland!
2. Three figures of men and Christians.
3. Foreigners and pilgrims, detach yourselves completely from here below, and travel quickly toward your homeland.
4. Do not let vain or dangerous thoughts settle in your mind.
5. While you have to interact with people, do not forget that paradise is your homeland.

GOSPEL OF THE SECOND SUNDAY AFTER EASTER

In a holy alliance

1. The Lord said: "Woe to the solitary man! For if he should fall, he has no one to lift him up."[1] And somewhere else: "*Funiculus triplex difficile rumpitur - A three-ply cord is not easily broken.*"[2] This means that a league of many tied together may not easily be broken.

The people of our century are feeble and need to show themselves to be powerful. To this end individuals join into societies, nations claim to be willing to join into alliances among themselves. Many times, however, the cement that binds them is not a divine one, consequently they soon break and fall to the ground powerless, unable to rise again. To be strong one must be bound to God, who is the strength by essence, and the eternal love.

Today Jesus claims to be the good shepherd who lays down his life for the sheep. He says that he knows all his sheep, and that these know him. He then adds: "Beware the hired hand who is no shepherd nor owner of the sheep - who catches sight of the wolf coming and runs away, leaving the sheep to be snatched and scattered by the wolf... I have other sheep that do not belong to this fold. I must lead them, too... There shall be one flock, then, one shepherd."[3]

---

[1] Eccl 4:10
[2] Eccl 4:12
[3] Jn 10: 11-16

Jesus Christ, the true Son of the Eternal Father, is our father and our shepherd. We have to adhere to him deeply. Let us join our hearts in a holy alliance with God and we will draw an unbeatable support from him. The Lord says in St. John's gospel: "I am the vine, you are the branches. He who lives in me and I in him, will produce abundantly, for apart from me you can do nothing."[1] Say this to everyone: what can a man do without God? Let us join the Lord in a holy alliance. Jesus Christ is the true vine that gives vigor to its branches so that they can produce abundant fruits.

2. A cry has been heard on earth. It crept out of hell inaudibly and spread then like a thunder over the earth to exclaim: "Down with the kingdom of Jesus Christ, long live the kingdom of Satan!" People, indeed, were quite terrified. Good people hastened to hold on to Jesus more intimately. The evil ones separated themselves completely from Jesus and joined together under the banner of Satan. The latter ones, unfortunately, are very many, since they include heretics, atheists, the faithless of our times. They pretend to be powerful yet they cannot do much, for they have no vigor sustaining them. In the meantime, since they cannot do anything else worse, they make fun of the Lord and grow bold in shouting, like the proud in the city of Babel, that the triumph of their alliance is touching heaven, and is omnipotent on earth.

Does the cry of the fools, perhaps, intimidate the eye of God? Or, perhaps, do those insane individuals, vile and betrayers, take away from the Almighty all his strength? Were all men here on earth going to abandon him, God would never the less cease being equally blessed, rich, and glorious. He is

---

[1] Jn 15: 5

the vine. Wouldn't the vine bother about its branches being cut off? It doesn't stop having all its vigor within!

3. There is Satan's alliance, that includes all human beings who have disowned the name of Jesus. We will constitute the alliance of the Lord's soldiers. We receive vigor from the vine who is the Divine Savior.

There are individuals among us who believe in the power of the Savior, yet keep in their heart the poison of mortal sin. They are united, yet mortally, like a dying branch. There are even more individuals who are united with God by a holy love, and these are like living branches that, drawing life from the vine, are able to bear very abundant fruits.

Ah, that the vigor of the charity of Jesus Christ may fill our hearts abundantly! Then the miracles of wonder will take place in our midst again as they were seen time after again in hosts of martyrs, of confessors, and in ranks of virgins. Now, who can impede us from being part of these groups? Jesus Christ is the vine for all the branches that remain attached to it.

4. This vine, that is Jesus Christ, has been planted on Mt. Calvary. It has been watered with infinite love with the blood of the incarnate Word. With infinite care this vine is displayed so that everyone may come and draw vigor from it. Could Jesus Christ have offered greater proofs of love?... No way, no way! If no special vigor of strength or action is given to our heart, it is always because of our fault not God's. We are the wretched ones who do not know how to, or do not want to stick to the Lord so willingly as he with immense affection longs for joining us to himself. If we find ourselves in fault, let us make up for it immediately and thus we will

grow in building up a holy alliance, that is unbeatable by the adversaries of our Crucified Lord.

5. For now let us be convinced whole heartedly that our help is nothing but Jesus Christ. Jesus grants the grace to do good. It is Jesus who does it. The branch draws from the vine the power to bear fruit and the very substance of the fruit itself. Take a look at the apostles and the apostolic individuals. God called them to himself as living branches. He inspired into them the power of miracles, the strength of the prophecies, and put into their hearts the vigor of zeal which, in turn, produced the abundant fruits of conversion of all nations. Thus the holy alliance of the faithful followers of the Savior was formed. It was formed by adhering to the vine of Jesus Christ and by receiving from his all the vigor to be able to operate.

6. You might object: if it is God who does everything in us, what is the purpose for us to struggle hard?... Does the branch struggle in drawing and transmitting the vigor of the vine into all its parts? You have your own free will. You may not accept this vigor of grace. If you accept it, you get merit for it. If you let this vigor be active, you will receive a great recompense for it. Spiders, yes spiders, are those who from the juice of a most healthy doctrine want to draw the poison of a subverting doctrine.

7. Let us be soldiers of Jesus Christ and let us move united in a holy alliance. Jesus Christ is, indeed, our strength. Let us make use of it, let us take advantage of it. There was a time when most noble knights, called the Knights of Jesus Christ and of the Holy Sepulcher, hastened to Jerusalem carrying the banner of Calvary, filled with the vigor and

charity of Jesus Christ. Miracles of bravery were seen. Various times they saved the Church of the divine Savior from very serious defeats. Do those strong knights still exist? I say it with tears: the unfortunate ones, little by little, separated themselves from Jesus and suffered shameful defeats.

My fellow companions, here we have the future of our alliance. We will be the winners if we remain attached to Jesus, and thus we say: "To God alone the honor and the glory!"[1] However, if we separate ourselves from him we will *ipso facto* perish, we will automatically collapse. In dying we will have to strike our chest and say: "The fault is all ours!"

REFLECTIONS

1. The strength in a holy alliance.
2. It comes from Jesus Christ. He is the everlasting vine.
3. We draw vigor from Jesus Christ by adhering to him in faith and in charity.
4. Jesus Christ longs for giving us vigor.
5. In granting it to us, he gives the very substance of strength to our hearts.
6. Our obligation is to cooperate.
7. Then we have to give glory to God for every good operation, and blame ourselves for any undertaking that failed.

---

[1] 1 Tm 1:17

GOSPEL OF THE THIRD SUNDAY
AFTER EASTER

The misery of a withered branch

1. Leave the sneerers of good alone. It is better that you pray for their conversion. What misery is awaiting them if they persevere in their evilness till the end! The Lord says in St. John's Gospel: "A man who does not live in me is like a withered, rejected branch, picked up to be thrown in the fire and burnt."[1] Terrible punishment! Do not ever envy sinners for the eternity. Jesus Christ says in today's Gospel: "I tell you truly: you will weep and mourn while the world rejoices; you will grieve for a time, but your grief will be turned into joy. You are sad for a time, but I will see you again; then your hearts will rejoice with a joy no one can take from you."[2]

So, be comforted, my brothers and sisters. Your joy will be overabundant one day. And so more miserable will be the lot of the wicked. These individuals, like withered branches, will be cut off the vine, thrown out of the vineyard and set to burn in hell. Let us take a look at this punishment that is the most terrible one indeed that a Christian may deserve when he maliciously separates himself from the vine which is Jesus Christ.

2. Look at a small branch of a vine and be horrified. If it remains attached to the vine, it produces fruits, but if it does not, and is cut off from it, here you have a useless thing good

---

[1] Jn 15:6
[2] Jn 16:20-23

113

for nothing. A branch of a pear tree, of an apple tree or of any other tree could be used to make utensils useful around the house. A branch of a vine, instead, is good for nothing but being thrown out to be burnt. Sinners who separate themselves from God are withered branches. Miserable, how miserable! They deserve nothing but the anger and disdain of the fire. So, when you see the wicked man prospering here on earth, do you envy him?

3. Pray for him with all your heart, otherwise you will see him one day thrown out of the vineyard of the divine Savior. Outside the Church of Jesus Christ, outside the bosom of a holy Mother, Blessed Mary, away from the arms of a merciful father, Jesus Christ. Plead for him, or you will see the wicked and useless branch kicked out of the friendship of the saints, out of the communion with the angels and left there, a wicked branch, so that everyone may curse it. How different will, then, be the lot of the wicked who, today, scorns the just of the Lord! What would happen if one of us found himself out of the vineyard as a withered branch? Let us think of this and be horrified for a beneficial purpose.

4. A sinner who is thrown out of the vineyard will wither fully. As long as a branch is attached to the vine, though dead, it still receives some kind of moisture of faith, it still retains a few green leaves of good deeds. Yet, when it is thrown out, then it dries up completely. Poor sinner! When he receives the sentence of condemnation, he will have lost every good. He will have nothing of whatever good he might have practiced in the early years of his life. Nothing of that habit of performing good deeds. He will have no chance at all of practicing any moral virtue.

The soil of his heart will be burned as the land of Mongibello, the soil of his heart will be in an extreme drought. Come now and tell me that the wicked man is enjoying plenty of good! Look at him at the time of his death, when he will be deprived of everything.

5. On that terrible moment sinners will be tied in bundles. The proud together, and the greedy and and the lustful ones as well as all the others. Tell me now if a bundle of witered branches can make any move. Likewise neither will sinners be able to perform any good deed. They have lost their freedom, they have lost the power to do any good. Bundles are easily thrown into the fire. You handle them with the pitchfork, turning them up and down until they are completely burned. Likewise sinners in hell will be lifted up and down by their tormentors, the devils, or turned over in the midst of the flames without any chance for them to complain about it. They are dry branches.

6. See now how a bundle of vine branches burn. They burn down to the bottom. And so do the damned ones in hell. With one difference, however, that a bundle of vine branches quickly turns into ashes, while sinners will never be consumed. Miserable, miserable ones! It hurts so much if the little finger of our hand is burned by embers. What about the sinners who will be burning like withered branches? Imagine it! More than once you yourselves had the experience of throwing a bundle of vine branches into a fire.

7. Did you observe it? A lively fire burns a bundle of dry branches in a moment. With the fury of the fire of hell the wicked will burn there, yet without being consumed. The fire will be kindled every time a new wicked one will be added to

it. The flames will envelope them with a horrible whistle as to penetrate their bone marrow. Thus the justice of the Lord will be carried out. Sinners will burn because, by separating themselves from Jesus, the vine that supplies the vigor of the true vine, they have committed a very vicious iniquity.

My brothers and sisters, let us all fear that. Yet, if we do not want to remain attached to Jesus Christ for the sake of the reward and life that he promises to give us, at least let us stick to him for the fear of the punishment that threatens us.

REFLECTIONS

1. Misery of a withered branch.
2. A withered branch of a vine.
3. The Christian who is thrown out of the vineyard that is the Church of Jesus Christ.
4. It is left there to dry all the way through.
5. Then it is bundled up with the proud or any other wicked ones.
6. It is thrown into the fire.
7. So that it may burn without ever being consumed.

GOSPEL OF THE FOURTH SUNDAY AFTER EASTER

Incredible absurdity, still true

1. The older we become, the more evil we have to witness with our own eyes, which is absurd, yet unfortunately it is true.

Years ago, if someone had told you that Christians would call on the kingdom of Satan on earth, that they would throng to acclaim him, that they would lay down so as to let the devil step on their backs, with indignation you would have exclaimed: "That's impossible, that's impossible!" Today we are forced to witness all this and we are horrified greatly by it. Poor wretched ones, who will save us? Who will save us?

We read in today's Gospel that Jesus, appearing to his disciples, told them that he was going to leave them by ascending to heaven. He told them also not to be afraid, because they themselves were going to join him at the proper time. He added that they should not fear about the world, for at his return, he was going to convince the world of sin for not believing in him.[1]

This is the absurdity of evil that we witness in our midst still today. It consists in denying our faith in Jesus Christ. One more very wicked absurdity is to call on Satan to walk heavily over men. It's incredible, yet true. Isaiah reproaches this excess when he says: "Those who order you to bow down, that they might walk over you, while you offered your back like the ground, like the street for them to

---

[1] See Jn 16:5-14

walk on."[1] Now you tell me that human iniquity is not too much. Men and Christians commit excessive evils which would be unbelievable were they not true.

2. There was the time when the world with astonishment looked at Valerian, the magnificent emperor of Rome, who, taken to Persia, had to accompany Sapore, the king of that nation, like a most vile soldier all the time, so that when Sapore wanted to mount his horse, Valerian was immediately at hand to bend his back for the king to step on as on a stool. Such a case of extreme disgrace is perhaps more unique than rare in history, and we look upon it with pity. Valerian did not submit to that degrading service out of his own will. He had to, because, after waging war on Sapore, he was defeated and had fallen into his hands.

The most unbelievable wonder is that men and Christians bend their backs so that Satan may walk on them. We wonder because they bend their backs without being forced, but deliberately. The devil knows that he cannot do that unless man consents to it. As a matter of fact the devil tells him: "Bend down." And the Christian does not object, nor resist or refuse. He immediately, if not with words, certainly in fact, which is the worst thing ever, submits and bends his back to the devil, and is happy that the devil walks back and forth on him at his pleasure. Heaven, heaven, what do you say in the sight of such excess, which I do not know whether it is more out of malice or insanity?

3. Notice one more excess of iniquity. The devil simply says to the Christian: "Bend down so that I can walk on you." He does not say anything else. What does the

---

[1] Is 51: 23

Christian do? He not only bends his back, but he even lays down on the ground. I mean that, after committing one sin, he immediately adds one more, and more, thereby laying on the ground so that a host of devils walk on him at their pleasure.

Let us give you this example. Suppose that a vile assassin who escaped the gibbet goes to the king's son and says to him: "Bend your head to the ground so that I may walk on your back." Seeing that the king's son heartily does so, tell me, don't you think that he should immediately be taken to his father's presence?

Shame on the Christians, who are the children of the King of heaven, when they submit to Satan, the liar and murderer since the beginning! Shame on those Christians who submit to Lucifer allowing him to do with them whatever he likes! This is the extreme of iniquity which would be thought to be impossible if it were not true.

4. Unfortunately something even worse is done. One could lay in a private property, in a yard or field. In this case very few people would be allowed to walk on his back. But that same individual may choose to lay on a public road. In this case he exposes himself to everyone's insults, treated as cumbersome mud. Everyone can step on him, everybody can get on him. Everyone, no one excluded, can trample upon his neck and spit on his face. Horrible thing! When you begin committing one mortal sin of the flesh, or a grave injustice out of greed, or a cruel sin out of pride, when you add one fall to another as it happens to people out of habit, then you lay down like the mud on the public street, happy that all the devils of hell insult you.

5. The excess of which we have talked so far makes the blood rush to our head and makes us shudder. What are

we going to do next? This for sure: whenever Satan presents us with an image of pride, an object of greed or any form of sensuality, let us dispel that evil temptation immediately. Isn't the devil an assassin? Isn't he a most infamous traitor among all? He certainly is. Well, then, when he shows up at the entrance of the house of our mind or of our heart, let us drive him out immediately with force. Traitors are never welcome not even for an instant. The infamous are banned for good.

If we allow Satan to come in, he will immediately set in and it will be difficult to get rid of him afterward. Miserable is our weakness, while we need someone who is going to reproach us consistently so that we will not submit to Satan.

On our part, we will never commit an excess like this of submitting before Satan. Never, never more. When you, O Jesus Christ, will return to convince the world of sin, what will happen to us if you had to convince us of having submitted our back to Satan? What would happen to us?

REFLECTIONS

1. An incredible absurdity, yet true.
2. The devil says to the Christian: "Bend down, so that I may walk over you", and the Christian bends down.
3. Not only does he bend down, he even lays down.
4. Not only does he lay down on private area, he does so in the mud of a public road.
5. What an excess! When Satan comes to seduce us, do we drive him back to hell?

GOSPEL OF THE FIFTH SUNDAY
AFTER EASTER

A Christian tempter

1. The divine Savior comes to us with the attitude of a loving father, who spreads out the treasure of his belongings, lets his children review them, pointing out to them what might be more profitable and necessary for them. Listen to him when he speaks, for he will draw tears of consolation from you.

Jesus said to his disciples: "I tell you truly: whatever you ask the Father, in my name he will give you. Until now you have not asked for anything in my name. Ask and you shall receive, that your joy may be full."[1]

This is the discourse of Jesus Christ, the true Son of the eternal Father. A wretched little fellow comes by, filled with pretension and maliciousness. He comes to meet the Most High almost as though to make fun of him. He comes with the attitude of a rebel, raising up high two hands stained with crimes, fixes his two ugly eyes accustomed to scorn, and with the sound of mocking irony ends up with saying: "Tell me, tell me who is this?" It is the image of the Christian who in asking from God does not prepare his soul first but comes by as one who wants to tempt the Lord. Let us observe him bit by bit, because the mocker deserves to be known well enough to be abhored accordingly.

---

[1] Jn 16: 23-24

121

2. Take the example of two sons who go to their father to ask for something. One of them approaches his father and arrogantly says: "Just set quickly before me the best food and clothes you have, for I do not intend to wait too long." What a presumptious way of asking! Doesn't this individual tempt directly the bounty or severity of his father? Who is he who dares to speak so to his pious and just father? The other son, who really does not care about it, does not speak to his father like his brother, yet goes and presents himself to him unseemingly dressed, with his hair ruffled, with a discontented and demanding face. This does say much directly, but in fact he looks like one who wants to make fun of his father.

Christians, if you approach God to plead with him with no better dispositions than these evil ones, please do not take one step, for you do not come to pray but to insult God.

3. We approach God right when we come to him with a pure eye, with a humble and mortified attitude. We have to remove from our mind the darkness of mortal sin. We have to remove as much as possible the darkening caused by deliberate venial sins. How can one look to heaven and distinguish heavenly things from earthly ones if he does not take care to clear up fully the eye of his mind? Besides, we must approach God with all the faculties of our soul. We must approach God with our companions, the senses of our body. Yet, if our will is attached to the things of the earth and our senses crave for their earthly pleasures, how can they be worthy in the presence of the Lord?

When you have prepared your look and set your person properly you have made what we refer to as the remote preparation to pray well. Then comes the immediate preparation. This consists in making the request intended. This must be done by presenting in order and truth all those good reasons for mercy and power on God's part, of misery and sicknesses on our part, as clearly as a poor man in rags and tatters does when he implores for help deeply buried in all his misfortunes. Praying with this disposition is a devout one. Otherwise it is the request of the tempter.

4. You might claim that as soon as you see a church you are able to recollect yourself, that as soon as you kneel before the Crucifix you are able to plead. Pay attention that what you say is true and not otherwise. Or isn't your disposition like the one of many who are in prayer as lifeless pillars? There are some people who come to holy Mass, but do not make a move of their lips to pray. Others attend benediction and stand there all the time. These individuals honor the Lord like the dead stones of the columns, which, being placed there, at least obey in sustaining the house of the Lord! If you are devout in this way, do not consider yourselves safe.

You will tell me that you truly pray, but aware that God knows your needs better than you do, you think that it is enough that you make a general request, not a specific one. I answer you that God is more pleased when you ask for specific favors. The blind man on the road to Jericho called on Jesus as follows: "Jesus, son of David, have pity on me!" Jesus questioned him: "What do you want me to do for you?" The blind man said: "That I may see." Then Jesus healed him.[1] He who wants to be listened to makes use of all means to obtain it. Isn't it, then, opportune for a man to employ all methods possible to him in order to achieve what he wants?

---

[1] Mk 10: 46-52

5. In this case we must make an observation. While we set our mind in asking from God a special grace, we must not linger on it so much that we would not then be able to let it go for any reason. It is good that we pray for a beneficial grace from God. Yet who assures us that the Lord is more willing to grant us another grace that may be more beneficial to us? A pilot who needs to supply his ship with provisions steers toward his set port, but if the wind pushes the ship toward another port, which perhaps is closer and certainly more furnished, wouldn't the pilot be a fool to insist on his first destination?

This, too, is a bit of news that is good to keep in mind, because it might help us. Other than this, there is no more important norm for good prayer. Have we understood the lesson? Well, then, let us remember it all the time: it is an excellent and necessary thing to pray as a devout Christian. To pray with the dispositions of a Christian tempter is the worst and most ruinous thing.

REFLECTIONS

1. A tempting Christian.
2. Two tempting children.
3. Good mind and good heart are needed for good prayer.
4. Before praying to God, we have to turn our attention to heaven.
5. Once this is done, it is good also to let oneself be carried by the wind of the divine inspirations and of heavenly grace.

GOSPEL OF THE SUNDAY
WITHIN THE OCTAVE OF ASCENSION

Get rid of fear!

1. There are many Christians today who look at the religious horizon of society. They see dark clouds gather, flashs of lighting increase, freezing storms threathening. They close themselves in the house like snails in their shells and moan: "Poor us! Miserable is the community of the Church!" What are you afraid of? Get rid of your fear! Didn't Jesus Christ foresee that all these wicked things would happen to his Church? Listen now to the text of the gospel.

"Jesus said to his disciples: 'When the Paraclete comes, the Spirit of truth who comes from the Father, and whom I myself will send from the Father, he will bear witness on my behalf. You must bear witness as well, for you have been with me from the beginning. I have told you all this to keep your faith from being shaken. Not only will they expel you from synagogues; a time will come when anyone who puts you to death will claim to be serving God! All this they will do to you because they knew neither the Father nor me. But I have told you these things that when their hour comes you may remember my telling you of them.'"[1]

It is not out of the ordinary that the faithful followers of the divine Savior have to be persecuted. As a matter of fact the Church is portrayed as a ship in the midst of waves that starts off in the calm and then procedes swiftly in the midst of the storms. It is compared to a threshing floor that needs the

---

[1] Jn 15: 26-27; 16: 1-4

wind to be purified everyday. It is a battlefield in which it is good to be every day always ready for the battle. We are here at home, so do not be afraid! The Lord says through his apostle St. Luke: "Fear him who who has power to cast into Gehenna after he has killed. Yes, I tell you, fear him."[1] So, get rid of all fear that comes from men! In our regard, let us only fear the Lord. Let us heartily fear him, because he is truly the one who can give us the worst punishment by ceasing to love us.

2. St. John Chrysostom, bishop of Constantinople, denounced greatly the vices of the great ones and opposed the scandals of the emperial court. With great anger the emperor assaulted St. John with the intent of doing him harm as much as possible. He threatened him with penalties, but St. John did not bother with them. The emperor had him put in jail, and St. John happily laughed about it. The emperor threathened to put him in exile, and St. John answered that the whole world was his homeland. St. John kept repeating to himself: "Only one thing I must fear, sin, for I know that sin makes God condemn me to the fires of hell."

How much must we fear sin! Imagine how God stretches his merciful right hand, holding men suspended over the abyss of hell. Imagine how the lions of hell rush at them with fury to bite the victim. Wouldn't you feel a great horror and thus heartily recommend yourselves to the Most High? Or if you saw a bold reckless individual spitting on the hand of the one who is trying to control him, would you still hold yourselves with patience?

I am waiting for you to realize this. Aren't you the ones who cause the most vile injuries against God, who

---

[1] Lk 12: 5

prophane him with blasphemies, who sadden him with sensualities? Don't you, then, fear that God might send you to the bottom? Ah, fear, fear, for he is the Almighty!

3. Down there, in the center of the earth, there is the Gehenna, the horrible abyss that swallows all the refuse of the earth, and the reflux of the filthiness of hell. It is a narrow abyss that contains all the damned, crushing them against one another greatly. It is a deep abyss to which tends the weight of millions of damned individuals, crushing them like grapes, with no chance to make a move. Finally Gehenna or hell is a dark well, horrible, closed to any ventilation.

Miserable us, who cannot stand staying in sultry air, or in the dark for more than an hour, when the light is so inviting for us to enjoy. What would happen to one of us if he fell into that abyss of filthiness and thick darkness? Think you now whether it is worthwhile to fear the threat of a man. Let us fear the threats of God by shunning sin, for this is what causes for us an irreparable ruin.

4. After all, what evil can men do to us? Nothing, unless God permits them to do so. Still God, by his very essence, and out of justice, has the power to punish one by casting him into hell. Imagine a powerful man holding a criminal from the top of a tower over a well, as we said before, crowded with dragons and serpents. How much that wretched man would fear falling into it, how much would he cry out for mercy!

Yet we are the one. Has God, perhaps, to work hard to punish us? That is what the Lord's justice calls for over and over again. Justice would have carried out the sentence already, if the mercy of the Most High had not cried out more insistently. However, we are so stubborn in not paying attention to the danger, inflexible to any weight of threat. How wretched we are if we do not plead intensely that God may save us in his mercy.

5. St. Francis Borgia always kept his eyes on the wide opened abyss of hell. He stared at it with utmost fear. He would become pale in his face and shake in all his body. He shook and made his little room shake as well. After a while he would come back to his senses, and like one who has been spared from the abyss of hell out of God's mercy, would exclaim: "Do men still think of vanities and enjoy themselves in any sort of sin? Oh, tell them to fear God, to be stricken with horror at the sight of hell!"

The venerable servant of God, John of Avila, was praying before the Blessed Sacrament on the vigil of the feast of Corpus Christi when Jesus appeared to him in the image of the divine Savior being scourged at the pillar, ready to be crowned with thorns. John was horrified and asked: "My Jesus, what is this that I see with my eyes?" Jesus responded: "These are the wounds caused to me by the sins of Christians!" The servant of God fainted out of compassion. Then, keeping grip of all his strengths, began shouting all over and to everyone: "Avoid sin, shun sin always, because sin wounds Jesus the savior to death!"

My brothers and sisters, let us detest the iniquity of sin at least just like servants avoid guilt for fear of the punishment. May heaven be pleased if we are determined to abhor sin as children who are sorry for hurting God our father. To feel sorry as a loving child is true contrition that by itself and joined to the desire of receiving the sacrament of reconciliation saves us from Gehenna, that is the abyss of hell upon which we have reflected so far.

REFLECTIONS

1. Fear not men!
2. Sin is the only thing to fear.
3. This iniquity makes one fall into the abyss of hell.
4. God is powerful in punishing.
5. Oh, let us cry out for mercy, as servants or as children, that God may spare us.

GOSPEL OF THE FIRST SUNDAY AFTER PENTECOST

Tenderness of a father

1. The Lord looked at his eternal blessedness. He saw himself eternally happy and wished to share his blessedness. In an excess of love he created man innocent. In an excess of love he still continues the great work of the sanctification of man here on earth. The prophet Ezekiel describes the tenderness of the Lord who, speaking to the soul, says: "You were stark naked. I passed again by you and saw that you were now old enough for love. So I spread the corner of my cloak over you to cover your nakedness. I swore an oath to you and entered into a covenant with you; you became mine, says the Lord God."[1]

Admirable tenderness! It goes along very well with today's Gospel. The Lord, to prove that he wants everyone to be saved, and that he has laid out a very smooth path, speaks as follows: "Be compassionate as your Father in heaven is compassionate. Do not judge, and you will not be judged. Do not condemn, and you will not be condemned. Pardon, and you shall be pardoned. Give, and it shall be given to you. Good measure, pressed down, shaken together, running over, will they pour into the fold of your garment. For the measure you measure with, it will be measured back to you."[2]

Good God, how great you are in your mercies! Could man hope for any better for his salvation? At least let us pay

---

[1] Ez 16: 7-8
[2] Lk 6: 36-38

attention to this ineffable tenderness which the Lords provides for the salvation of his children, and let us be comforted in our heart.

2. Think of a woman of royal origins who has left the royal palace, gone out to the public square and is now roaming the fields contesting with the pigs for a few acorns. What a misery and what a shame! The king comes out hunting and sees the run-away woman, hiding behind the leaves like the sinful Eve. The king gives her a merciful glance as to say: "I forgive you... come back..." Then he comes close to her, covers her with his mantle to protect her from cold. Repentance is already taking over her heart. She begins to love her benefactor. The king grants her his covenant of friendship, then makes an oath to marry her, and finally he wants her to be totally his.

Admirable encounter! It is the encounter of God with a sinful soul. The Lord begins by granting her a loving glance, then he makes her hear his voice saying: "Come!" If the soul consents, God offers his nuptial oath, and finally he takes her into marriage as far as to say: "You are all mine". Thus he establishes the foundation of an intimate friendship, of a loving and lasting covenant.

Here we have to contrast who is the God who comes searching for and who is the sinful man who has run away. From this contrast the immense tenderness of God our Father will emerge better.

3. Let us take a scriptural event as an example. Let us look at the case of Mary Magdalene. This woman was a public sinner, the prostitute of Magdala, all pompous in her long trains of dresses, her head crowned with roses. Lovers ran after her seeking their great enjoyment. Yet, while men

flattered her so much, how miserable and disgraceful she looked in the sight of God! And the Lord had pity on her. He came, stopped by and turned to her one of those looks which he later gave to Peter, and to Matthew, which made them turn to him. The mind of Mary Magdalene began to clear up, her heart to repent. She saw the horrible evil she had done, and began to cry. Fortunate Magdalene! Fortunate is our soul if she is eager to listen to the divine inspirations and follow them.

4. At the very moment Mary Magdalene broke into tears she was justified. A father starts with looking with eyes of compassion at his son who has committed a grave fault. The child becomes upset, his eyes become full of tears and begins to sob bitterly. At this point the father embraces his son, prompts him to quiet down, to forget the past, for he is completely forgiven now. The father exhorts him to look at the future, and thus he will be doubly dear to him.

Likewise Jesus Christ with Mary Magdalene. As soon as he saw love in her tears, he covered her with the mantle of justification. He then kept defending her against the Pharisee who recognized her as an infamous woman, and said: "I tell you, that is why her many sins are forgiven -- because of her great love." Jesus, then, turned to Mary herself and gave her the comfort which alone could console her desolate heart. He said to her: "*Remittuntur tibi peccata tua - Your sins are forgiven.*"[1] What a consolation for a soul that pines for the evil of so many sins committed!

5. Let us go on with the case of Mary Magdalene. The fortunate one, as soon as she heard that Jesus had forgiven

---

[1] Lk 7: 47-48

her, every day she tried to get closer and closer to him. She was happy when she could listen to the discourses that came from his lips. She kept every single word of his with religious care, thus preparing herself to merit that Jesus would make with her the covenant of a holy friendship. Mary Magdalene consented and thus she remained faithful everafter, thinking of nothing but of having Jesus in her heart and mind. She defied the scorn of the Jews at the time of the passion of her Savior. She defied the threats of the soldiers on the way to and at the foot of the cross on Mt. Calvary. She defied the guards armed for the custody of the sepulcher of Jesus, thus showing to the end of how grateful she was for the immense benefit granted to her by Jesus by calling her to himself.

6. Finally Jesus chose Mary Magdalene to be totally his, by leading her not only to an outstanding degree of holiness, but also to a reward of admirable trust. After his resurrection, Jesus appeared first to Mary Magdalene and said to her: "Go to my brothers, my disciples, and tell them what you have seen, that Jesus has risen from the dead." Mary Magdalene hastened to carry the messages of her Savior and helped to save souls. Later Jesus called her to leave Judea and travel to Marseilles to seclude herself in solitude. She obeyed promptly, and there in Marseilles she lived for forty more years in a most loving conversation with her Lord.

Souls who have begun to love the Lord, do you like today's lesson? Put it into action, then. Sinful souls who laid naked and disgraceful, tell me, how were you covered with the mantle of virtue? How much do you rejoice in your heart? You yourselves, tell everyone how admirable is the tenderness which God our father shows to his loved ones.

REFLECTIONS

1. Tenderness of a father.
2. God first calls a soul from the abyss of her misery.
3. Then he takes her to himself as he did with the sinful Magdalene.
4. How he made an oath of friendship with her.
5. In this state a soul enjoys giving proofs of fidelity.
6. Until God calls her to become totally his.

GOSPEL OF THE SUNDAY WITHIN THE OCTAVE OF CORPUS CHRISTI

Who thinks of the Lord?

1. The Lord is all for our soul. He has created us. He has redeemed us. He has prepared a place of glory in his paradise. Yet who thinks of the Lord?

We read in the holy Gospel something that really frightens us. Here is how the evangelist St. Luke puts it: "Jesus said to his disciples: A man was giving a large dinner and he invited many. At dinner time he sent his servant to say to those invited, 'Come along, everything is ready now.' But they began to excuse themselves, one and all. The first one said to the servant, 'I have bought some land and must go out and inspect it. Please excuse me.' Another said, 'I have bought five yoke of oxen and I am going out to test them. Please excuse me.' A third said, 'I am newly married and so I cannot come.' The servant returning reported all this to his master. The master of the house grew angry at the account. He said to his servant, 'Go out quickly into the streets and alleys of the town and bring in the poor and the crippled, the blind and the lame.' The servant reported after some time, 'Your orders have been carried out, my lord, and there is still room.' The master, then, said to the servant, 'Go out into the highways and along the hedgerows and force them to come in. I want my house to be full, but I tell you that none of those invited shall taste a morsel of my dinner.'"[1] So much for now for the holy Gospel.

Think about this yourselves and ask: who thinks of the Lord? They do not even pay attention to him when God invites them to share the great enjoyment of a dinner, wonder how they will think of him when they are called to a bench to defend the honor and the glory of his religion! Writing to the Philippians, St Paul openly complains when he says: "Everyone is busy seeking his own interests rather than those of Christ Jesus."[2] Most bitter reproach! Let us look into it part by part to at least learn how to correct ourselves.

2. Here again, think of a rich man and a good father, who does everything for his employees, is wholeheartedly for his children. At the same time, those employees think of nothing but taking advantage enjoying themselves, spending their time in idleness, seeking their own interests and not at all the interests of their employer and father. Poor master! Add to it what the children do to dissipate their father's properties rather than adding to them! Unfortunate father, how brokenhearted he must be!

God himself is that master and father. The servants he rules are all faithful in general, that is those Christians who in a body do not profess to being intimate with Jesus. How much do these neglect the honor of the Lord! Thus they offend him even more. There are also others who, like beloved children, have dedicated themselves to his service, who have been consecrated for his ministry, and even these are found to be seeking their own interests rather than the glory of Jesus

---

[1] Lk 14: 16-24
[2] Phil 2:21

Christ. O children, children, how much do you yourselves displease the Most High!

3. See yourselves your evil heart. If someone says an offensive word to you, you answer back immediately, you demand an apology immediately. As regard to God, do you ever hear an injurious blasphemy or see the affront of a scandal? Facing the ever so many absurdities you happen to witness, how many times were you eager to defend the honor of the Lord? As you know how to care for your honor, so you know how to defend your belongings. If one steals grapes from your vineyard, you resent it. If someone brings any damage to your field, you expect them to make reparation for it.

Yet while you act so quickly for your own interests, how do you handle God's interest? Do you hold dear to you the poor of Jesus Christ? Do you care for the widows and the orphans? Are you, at least, able to curb the sinners if you are not able to convert them? How much do you care in intervening against the doom of the churches which are the house of the Lord?... Or do you belong to the number of those who take advantage of the goods of the Church for their own sake in drawing contracts and running public businesses?

Find out now how wise individuals seek the interests of the glory of God. Take a look at what only you can do, and then state whether God has no real reason to complain that men seek their own interests and do not look for the glory of Jesus Christ.

4. Worse still. Aren't there Christians who pretend to be religious to do better business? There are some who kiss the crucifix to secure for themselves a political post; there are others who go to Mass, but only to avoid being convicted in

some affair. There is even someone who wears the ecclesiastical robe and attends public functions, but for the only purpose to disguise his usuries and hide his depravities. What an excess! They make use of God to sin more easily. Could one ever say that these persons think of the Lord? They think of him, yes, but only to hurt him.

5. So, what are we supposed to do? This for sure, feel bad for the very many injuries brought against God. In order, then not to give the impression that we say one thing while we think the opposite, let us conduct ourselves in such a way before initiating any speech or action to examine whether or not it brings glory to God. If our heart says that it does so, then we put ourselves into it lovingly. If our heart tends to deceive us, then let us correct ourselves. St. Ignatius of Loyola kept saying: *"Omnia ad maiorem Dei gloria - everything for the greater glory of God"*, and with this consistent motto in his heart and on his lips he was able to happily please God and make reparation for the numberless injuries brought to the glory of God by the numerous heresies of the past century.

6. For this noble purpose I want to give you an example. St. Joseph is rightly considered being the first among all saints. He was so because, being chosen to be the spouse of the Virgin Mary, he made use of his role only for the glory of God. He was the foster father of Jesus, but only for the purpose of covering the ineffable mystery of the incarnation. In his life he appeared only a few times, when he sought the honor of the Lord. After death, his name remained unkown for many centuries, until the glory of God saw to it that it became more known. In everything else, for the glory of God, St. Joseph endured not a few hardships, toils, dangers

and even manifest persecutions, as it happened in Judea and in Eypt.

St. Joseph, indeed, was a faithful guardian of divine honor! He rightly deserves to be chosen by each one of us as a protector in waging the battles of the Lord. Let us choose him as our advocate and defender so that we may protect ourselves and defend ourselves from the senses which seek their own comfort at the cost of even bringing injury to the honor of Jesus Christ.

REFLECTIONS

1. Who thinks of the Lord?
2. All people think of themselves.
3. They care for their own honor and for their riches, not for God's.
4. Under the pretext of God's glory, they even take advantage of it to give vent to their own whims.
5. Who feels sorry for the large number of injuries brought to God?
6. Let us feel bad about it and do something about it with the right intention as St. Joseph, spouse of Mary, and the chaste foster father of Jesus, did.

GOSPEL OF THE THIRD SUNDAY AFTER PENTECOST

An example of divine patience

1. We gaze around and see a growing crowd of very wicked Christians, offensive to God, enemies of the country, noxious to human society. We find some of them to look like devils with flesh and blood who threaten to sink the religious and civil order. Horrified, we turn our gaze on high and pray: "Lord, why don't you command that the earth open up for them to fall into the abyss when these wicked ones come by?..." Yet, how foolish we are!... Who among us has ever known the limitless bounty and kindness of God? At the same time can we deny that the Lord has been somehow extremely patient with us? Why has he let us live as sinners? "Do you not know that God's kindness is an invitation to you to repent?", writes St. Paul.[1]

In today's Gospel we read what I am going to talk about: "The tax collectors and sinners were all gathering around to hear him, at which the Pharisees and the scribes murmured, 'This man welcomes sinners and eats with them.' Then he addressed this parable to them: 'Who among you, if he has a hundred sheep and loses one of them, does not leave the ninety-nine in the wasteland and follow the lost one until he finds it? And when he finds it, he puts it on his shoulders in jubilation. Once arrived home, he invites friends and neighbors in and says to them: Rejoice with me, because I have found my lost sheep. I tell you, there will likewise be more joy in heaven over one repentant sinner than over

---

[1] Rom 2:4

ninety-nine righteous people who have no need to repent. What woman, if she has ten silver pieces and loses one, does not light a lamp and sweep the house in a diligent search until she has retrieved what she lost? And when she finds it, she calls in her friends and neighbors to say, 'Rejoice with me! I have found the silver piece I lost.' I tell you, there will be the same kind of joy before the angels of God over one repentant sinner."[1]

So do not wonder why God lets sinners live longer on earth. He lets them live so that they may finally repent. This is a case of divine patience as I am going to briefly show you.

2. Let us take a look at something which often takes place within a family. Think of a father who does everything for the sake of his children. Three of these hang around in the house without giving much consolation. They misbehave, and even rebel. You cannot even imagine how much the father struggles to get them back in line for the peace of the family. His caresses to them being of no avail, he has to resort to threats. He even punishes them, yet he does so with the love of a father who is willing to forgive.

The three youths take the punishment with various attitudes. The first one is aware of the good intention of his father, yet he still remains insensitive, thereby he is ungrateful. The second one is aware too, yet he not only does not repent, but makes fun of his father. This child is not only ungrateful, he is wicked indeed. The third one takes the punishment, convinced that it does not come from a good heart, and so he gets angry at his father even more. This child belongs to the number of those who are hopeless.

---

[1] Lk 16: 1-10

Let us now make our application. That loving father is God himself, our lord. How hurt he is seeing how many of his children disobey him! To make them repent, he speaks gently to their hearts, and if this is not enough, he punishes them with inner grief, or physical diseases, illnesses and deprivations. How do Christians react to him? There are some who do not realize how God, through punishments, is trying to save them. These Christians seem to be desperate at this point. There are others who understand what God is doing, yet they scorn him or remain indifferent. Oh Christians, wake up! Don't you realize that he who is punishing you is the Lord, and he does so for your sake? A good father is not the one who abandons his misbehaving child, but the one who scolds him so as to make him repent.

3. Take a better look at this. Isn't it a great benefit and admirable kindness on God's part to wait for a long time so that a wicked son of his has time to repent? God could send him to hell quickly, who does not know that? Yet he waits while enduring so many injuries and iniquities from men.

Any individual, though a good one, resents repeated injuries. A father, though loving, resents rebellion from his children. The Lord, who is much greater, bears with them. How do you feel about it? Heavens wonder in distress, the earth is astonished. The angels of heaven and the just on earth join their voices in singing: "The mercies of the Lord have no limits."

Yet, if Christians do not surrender to this excessive divine mercy, what should we say?... Their ingratitude and blindness is monstrous indeed.

4. More so, if you contrast with that the kindness which the Lord shows in order to draw his children back to

himself. I give you an example taken from Scripture. Jesus Christ kept Judas Iscariot among his apostles for three years. He fed him at his table, taught him with his preaching, edified him with his divine examples. He even gave him a special sign of kindness by entrusting him with the care of the apostolic group's money. The divine Savior was good in covering up at home for the defects of Judas so that he might repent, always speaking well with strangers about him so that they would not lose esteem for him. What did he not do at the last Supper, when for the first time he shared his most holy Body, the incarnate Word, with all his disciples and Judas himself? And when in the garden of Gethsemani, all covered with bloody sweat, he came to him and said to him: "My friend, you too?...", and offered his lips for the kiss?... At the showing of these acts of kindness even the heart of a tiger would have become tamed. Not the heart of Judas! The more Jesus showed him kindness, the more Judas took advantage of it for his own wicked intent, for his proud ambition, so far as to end miserably as I am horrified in hinting at, but you know very well. What do you think of it now?

I appeal to you, good fathers, family-heads. When you have employed every care to set a child of yours on the right track, and see that he becomes more wicked to straying away from it, you are shocked in your mind, hurt in your heart. Patience becomes slim little by little. You are almost going to curse the child who makes you age before time and opens the grave for you before time.

Now you think that the Lord is little hurt in seeing a sinner become as insolent in his sins as he becomes aware of how good God is? How wicked it is to abuse the kindliness of the Most High by sinning!... Now we do not understand very well, but one day we will understand it clearly.

5. After all, will God bear with you for a long while here on earth? Do you know for how long? An earthly father, though good, ends up by losing his patience. A friend, though dear, if he finds you to be hopeless, leaves you. Human beings as they are, these individuals should not be offended by the ungratefulness that comes from their equals, yet they complain about it. Will God not complain, when he knows that a sin committed against him is a sin of infinite malice? It is less evil to lack respect for a brother of ours within the family than lacking respect for the bishop of our diocese, worse still for the pope of the entire world! What, then, about lacking respect due to the Most High?... Have no doubt, God punishes... God does punish.

Who can assure you that the Lord is going to bear with you even until tomorrow?... If he wishes to punish you immediately, does he lack the power to do so? Or has he no abyss to hurl you into, from which you will not be able to come out any more? Let us fear the Lord, then, let us fear him at the very hour he is good to us. Let us fear the Lord, because as he is benevolent in waiting, so he will be severe in judging us.

REFLECTIONS

1. An example of divine patience.
2. Three examples of human malice.
3. All along the Lord waits with kindness.
4. And he employs all his cares of divine mercy.
5. However, if we do not surrender to him, that heavenly kindness, waiting in vain for us, will turn into an anger of greatest punishment.

GOSPEL OF THE FOURTH SUNDAY AFTER PENTECOST

The arrows of the Lord

1. The soldiers of Hanibal, Caesar or Napoleon are praised so much because at the command of their captains they dashed like arrows to frighten the earth. What are they compared to the apostles and apostolic people, soldiers of the Lord, who like arrows in the hands of Christ have gone and still go through the earth? Are the prodigious undertakings of these men duly praised?

First of all, listen to the account of the Gospel. The divine Savior wanted to draw to himself a few men who, motivated by him, would go all over the world. He acted as it is recounted by St. Luke:

"As Jesus stood by the lake of Genesareth, and the crowd pressed in on him to hear the word of God, he saw two boats moored by the side of the lake; the fishermen had disembarked and were washing their nets. He got into one of the boats, the one belonging to Simon, and asked him to pull out a short distance from the shore; then, remaining seated, he continued to teach the crowds from the boat. When he had finished speaking he said to Simon, 'Put out into deep water and lower your nets for a catch.' Simon answered, 'Master, we have been hard at it all night long and have caught nothing; but if you say so, I will lower the nets.' Upon doing this they caught such a great number of fish that their nets were at the breaking point. They signaled to their mates in the other boat to come and help them. These came, and together they filled the two boats until they nearly sank. At the sight of this, Simon Peter fell at the knees of Jesus saying, 'Leave me, Lord. I am a sinful man.' For indeed, amazement at the catch they had made seized him and all his shipmates, as well as James and John, Zebedee's sons, who were partners with Simon. Jesus said to Simon, 'Do not be afraid. From now on you will be catching men.' With that they brought their boats to land, left everything, and became his followers."[1]

Thus they became soldiers in the hands of Jesus Christ, and they became very skilfull archers in drawing souls to God. Referring to them, the Psalmist had already written in spirit: "Like arrows in the hand of a warrior are the sons of one's youth."[2] Let us look at these prodigious arrows of valiant soldiers and let us ponder upon how much they are able to operate in the hands of God.

2. Peter, James and John, as well as all the others who followed the divine Savior, were all busy with their nets in their fishing trade. Jesus comes by and shakes them up saying: "Do you realize that the world is in Satan's hands?... Rise and go so that you may drive him out and stir the nations to salvation." This divine call was enough. Those men left the dirt of earthly possessions then and there and never thought about them as long as they lived. They saw to it that they kept up with the invitation of the Savior. They went through and eventually saved the earth, as you well know. Shaken up by Jesus, the apostles then shook us. We are the fortunate children of those valiant archers, and we now sing the hymn of jubilation and our salvation.

Shaken by Jesus Christ, the apostles never more feared the shocks coming from philosophers and pagan judges, that

---

[1] Lk 5: 1-11
[2] Ps 127 (126): 4

is the furor of people who rejected their teachings. All the just on earth are now the children of the apostles. They are shaken by God and called to become shakers. Do you like the noble role assigned to you by the Lord? To this purpose listen to what one of your companions alone, one of the apostolic individuals, did. I want to talk about St. Francis Xavier.

3. He was attending to his beloved studies at the University of Paris looking for making a name for himself in the world when St. Ignatius shocked him by saying: "What matters if you gain the first place on earth and you lose your soul at the end? There are so many pagans to be instructed, so many souls to be saved..." Thus St. Ignatius skillfully talked to him about the situation in the world. St. Francis burned with zeal and responded: "Well, I want to be an arrow in the hands of God."

St. Francis went to Rome and said to the Pope: "I want to be an arrow in the hands of God. I want to travel through the whole world to bring back to the feet of the Cross all the people who are still away from it." Thus he stopped caring for profane studies as well as for what his companions said. He did not even take a step to kiss his elderly mother good-bye. St. Francis dashed like an arrow to target souls and take them back to Christ.

4. In an instant the arrow travels the entire earth. St. Francis Xavier traveled so much in order to save soul. The actual distance he traveled was four times the distance around the earth. As soon as he heard from the lips of his superior that God wanted him for the infidels, he flew to them. To be quicker, he took along only the breviary and a staff for the rest of his life, that is ten years.

Let us compare ourselves to him now. Are we willing to leave everything behind in order to save one soul? Do we run swiftly without being hindered by family obstacles or attractive comforts? Ah, we are something else! To save a soul, we do not take the pain of undertaking a long journey, but we limit ourselves just to say a word to reprimand the audacity of a blasphemer.

5. Let us proceed. St. Francis was a most straight arrow. He never bent right or left. He sought the conversion of people and he got it. He did not allow himself to be sidetracked by deprivations, dangers, honors or persecutions. You would see him being a servant with servants to convert them, ignorant with the ignorant, wise with the wise, only with the intent to lead them to salvation. If needed for the salvation of souls, one day he would approach the people infected with the pestilence, or enter the factories or join the workers in the fields. Leaving from there, if requested, he would willingly carry a noble message and receive princely honors, yet he would go back to his previous modest duties on the following day. He aimed at one thing only: to save souls, who cared for anything else? Thus lived St. Francis; while we do not achieve much because we allow ourselves to be taken over in our minds by our self-love.

6. St. Francis cared less for himself. He also disdained the advice of all those who opposed him urging him not to do so much or at least not to hurry so much. Before he departed, there was someone who warned him about the dangers by land or by sea recently found out. He did not pay attention to them. He did not fear any difficulties in the land of infidels. He went to meet the bite of serpents, as well as death presenting itself in the image of the people infested with the

plague. No one was ever able to enter the Chinese empire, yet St. Francis got close to it and died at its threshold. This is the determination to serve God!... Compared to such an example what can we answer?... Ah, we let ourselves be won over by any little difficulty! We quickly come up with arguing that it is not prudent to do something that exceeds the common expectation.

7. St. Francis was an arrow that pierced deep into the hearts. His words were like a battle. By the thousands the souls of the pagans fell before him. It suffices to say that he personally baptized one-million-two-hundred-thousand individuals. Yet he prepared a much greater number of people to be baptized by others, because he always longed for greater conquests. Those who fell won over by his words remained the strongest ones. Five kings prostrated themselves before the cross of the Savior. St. Francis Xavier joined such a care of zeal and fire of love to his words that one who approached him once was taken forever. What a noble warrior St. Francis Xavier was! What about us?... Ah, we are not able to enter anyone's heart, because we have not let the arrows of the grace of the Lord penetrate our innermost selves.

8. An arrow is powerful when it is hurled by a powerful arm. God must hurl us. On our part, however, we are seriously in bad shape. We do not allow ourselves to be hurled. We set obstacles to the grace of the Lord. We set obstacles to the will of the superior. We want only what satisfies us, consequently how can God make use of an instrument that refuses to lend its cooperation? Here too we see truth on God's part and utmost shame on ours. After all we achieve so little for the glory of the Lord because we do not allow the Lord to make use of us as he would like.

REFLECTIONS

1. The arrows of the Lord are powerful.
2. Arrows of the Lord are the just individuals and above all the apostolic ones.
3. Like the apostles and St. Francis himself, these leave everything.
4. They quickly travel through the earth.
5. They proceed straight without bending right or left.
6. They overcome all difficulties.
7. And strike deeply.
8. Because they allow themselves to be handled fully by God.

GOSPEL OF THE FIFTH SUNDAY
AFTER PENTECOST

A half-way Christian?

1. In the early times of the Church it was considered morally good that when a Christian woman married a non-christian man, one of the main objectives of the fervent woman would be to turn her fervent spouse to the foot of the cross of Jesus. The good daughters of the Lord were able to quickly achieve their intent, thereby obtaining the spreading of the holy faith and of the kingdom of Jesus Christ. However, if a wife delayed in obtaining the conversion of her husband, there was anguish within and without the family. They stared at the face of the unfortunate woman with sadness, saying: "That woman is a half-way Christian".

After so many centuries of Christianity do we still find half-way Christians?... It is sad to mention it. How many, oh, how many there are!... They do not observe their duties toward God, nor do they observe their duties toward men. Listen to how the divine Savior complains about this in today's Gospel, how he throws his threats. Listen to it attentively and let all be horrified by it.

"Jesus said to his disciples: I tell you, unless your holiness surpasses that of the scribes and Pharisees you shall not enter the kingdom of God. You have heard the commandment imposed on your forefathers, 'You shall not commit murder; every murderer shall be liable to judgment.' What I say to you is: everyone who grows angry with his brother shall be liable to judgment; any man who uses abusive language toward his brother shall be answerable to the

151

Sanhedrin, and if he holds him in contempt he risks the fires of Gehenna. If you bring your gift to the altar and there you recall that your brother has anything against you, leave your gift on the altar, go first to be reconciled with your brother, and then come and offer your gift."[1] Thus far, the holy Gospel.

Now I am going to ask you: can a half-way Christian feel secure?... Not at all. The same St. Luke comes forward to tell us: "Whoever puts his hand to the plow but keeps looking back is unfit for the reign of God."[2] Most dreadful sentence! To understand it we will examine it part by part right now.

2. The divine Savior was preaching in the fields of Judea when a young man approached him and said: "Teacher, I want to follow you wherever you go and forever, but let me go home to settle all my affairs first." Jesus looked at him with compassion and told him these severe words: "Whoever puts his hand to the plow but keeps looking back is unfit for the reign of God." Most dreadful words! By reign of God we mean the one that is already here on earth where we have to work, or we mean the kingdom of heaven. Now he who puts his hand to a good deed but he does not complete it, is not fit either for the kingdom of Christ on earth or for the kingdom of Christ in heaven. What a terrible discourse! Yet this is so also in human affairs.

Alexander the Great had in his army a soldier by the same name Alexander, but he was a timid and lazy soldier. Alexander the Great told him once: "I expect of you one of two things: either you change your name or you must leave

---

[1] Mt 5: 20-24
[2] Lk 9:62

my army." It is expected that a soldier resembles his captain, a son resembles his father.

3. The young man would have been accepted for the apostolate, but because he kept his heart divided in two, in between his love for Jesus and the love for his earthly affairs at home, he was immediately rejected. Whoever enters the apostolate, becomes part of a very valuable enterprise. He has to plow, that is the most important act. He has to cut straight furrows in the soil, that is, he has to do something that cannot be obtained by those who look backward.

Pay attention to the rule that Jesus set in choosing his apostles. He first speaks to Peter, to James and to John and sees that they immediately leave everything to follow him. To Matthew counting his money at the collector's desk he says: "Follow me", and immediately Matthew follows him like a child. Jesus was pleased with such as these in a very special way. Jesus called them to be his apostles. In regard to the young man mentioned in this case, since Jesus found him to be still attached to earthly things, he told him immediately that he was unfit for the reign of God. How confounded we should be finding ourselves still so attached to the things of earth!

4. Then you are going to hear a threat like lightning. The Lord says: "Whoever puts his hand to the plow but keeps looking back is unfit for the reign of God." What does this mean?... With no doubt it means this, that if the Lord inspires us to do a good deed which we intend to do but never decide to get to it because of difficulties we encounter along the way, this does not justify us before God.

Imagine that a master says to his servant: "Till my garden, since it is full of briars." And the servant answers:

"Yes, sir!" But, then, coming to his task he is scared by it and ends up falling asleep in the midst of the garden, what would you say of such a worker? Here I reason this way: if we believe that God expects of us such a deed, why don't we tackle it willingly and immediately?... Or if we believe that we have been called because we feel so in our heart, but at the same time we doubt that God can and is willing to give us his assistance, then where is our faith?

What a tragedy!... Perhaps still today God calls so many to be Aarons and Moseses to lead his people, to wipe the tears of so many oppressed, to untie so many fetters of slavery, yet since those who are called do not believe, they do not carry out the call. What a tragedy for those who are being called, what damage for the souls who could be saved through them in the midst of so many toils of the Church!...

5. When God calls us to spiritual tasks, we must not even look at the obstacles of earthly things or the difficulties that might ensue. Those who do pay attention to the difficulties end up making a most hateful comparison. They say to themselves: "Is it better for me to dedicate myself to the things of God or to the things of the world? That I think of heaven or of the earth?..." This kind of comparison, though made in passing and with a simple thought, results in being so disgusting to God that he finds him who thinks himself unfit for the very important business of his glory, for the noble task of his apostolate.

Furthermore, it is more marvelous than rare for one to look at earthly things and not get himself attached to them. He looks at the earth, seeks it, and becomes a slave of it. What he gets from the earth, if he can, is the recompense which the soul only wants for herself.

6. Fear grows more at this point in reflecting that the Lord here speaks in general. He says: *"Nemo mittens... No one who puts his hand to... unwilling..."* Anyone, then, from the clergy or laity, from those who are in the apostolate or in the regular life... any man or woman among Christians who, called to do a work of good, become fearful and do not respond to the call, any of them falls into the consequences of the divine threats! God wants his followers to be strong, his Christians to be constant, to be steadfast and persevering to the end.

Go now, and excuse if you can today's wishy washy Catholics, who talk a lot claiming that they must do plenty of things, speak up, but then they are the first ones withdrawing within themselves as the snail retreats into its shell at the appearance of the first danger.

7. Are these, then, the soldiers of Christ Jesus?... They are unfit for the battle. Are these the plowers meant to challenge the heat of the spring sun and the weariness of the seasons?... They cannot face the troubles. Since they are unfit to fight, or to work, likewise they are not able to defend themselves so as not to die, unable to gather a grain of wheat so as not to starve. They will collapse in defeat. They will die of starvation! Good Lord, what will happen to me? What will happen to so many Christians of today, what will happen, what?...

8. Is there anything worse still?... There are individuals who set out willingly for a good undertaking, but then they quit. At the first encounter with difficulties, they feel lost. At the first assaults they surrender and withdraw. Viles, viles!... If they do not give themselves actually to worldly life, they go back to it with their hearts, which is equally wrong. Viles,

viles! These are traitors of a holy cause. Viles, viles! You have before yourselves the honor of Jesus Christ. You face the good of your soul. You behold the reward of paradise and you do not care in any way? Go forward, go forward or you will be vile forever! Forward until death! A half-way Christian cannot possibly be saved!

REFLECTIONS

1. Half-way Christian?
2. Whoever is called by the Lord to the apostolate is expected to respond immediately.
3. He, whose heart is divided between God and earthly things, is unfit for the reign of God.
4. Once an undertaking is made possible, it must be carried out immediately.
5. With no regard to difficulties or hardships.
6. Whoever is not generous and firm is never safe.
7. For he is unfit for the reign of God.
8. Still, less fit are those who, after embracing a vocation, withdraw in fact or in their desire.

GOSPEL OF THE SIXTH SUNDAY
AFTER PENTECOST

A beneficial medicine

1. Here on earth, and specifically in our midst, there is a mystery which can be hardly understood by most of us. It is the mystery of life's tribulations. Pagans were even scandalized by this and said: "Isn't God unjust in burdening man with so many sufferings?..."

Among Christians above all there are individuals who do not know of the mysteries of the cross of the Savior, and so they say: "Why should man be subjected to so many tribulations?" Unfortunately, these wretched individuals do not realize that they are sick and in need of tribulations indeed. Life's tribulations are medicines for human infirmities. What medicines and how suitable, indeed!...

We read in the holy Gospel that a multitude of people went to listen to the divine Savior. So eager were they not to miss a parable of Jesus' discourses, they followed him for three days by the lake or up in the mountain. Willing to listen to him so much, they bore not a few hardships, especially hunger. Couldn't Jesus help them out on the spot?... Surely he could, who does not know that?, yet he waited for the third day. Realizing that the crowds were becoming exhausted, he took five loaves and two fish, blessed and broke them and gave them to feed the people. All those present ate their fill. The fragments remaining, when gathered up, filled twelve baskets.[1]

---

[1] Mt 14:13-21

Thus the Lord satisfied a lengthy hunger. Yet, first he wanted them to endure tribulation. Tribulation is the medicine for human passions. The Lord says in the *Book of Sirach*: "Accept whatever befalls you, in crushing misfortune be patient; for in fire gold is tested, and worthy men in the crucible of humiliation."[1] This passage from the *Book of Sirach* is like a massive treasure in a rich mine. Better still, it is like the substance of a salutary medicine. Let us ponder on the value of this medicine. Tribulation is a most useful medicine to cure human passions.

2. All of us have headaches. Oh, that smoke of pride, the attachment to the earth and that venom of concupiscence that intoxicate us! Yet are we likewise willing to take the medication? There are sick people who, serious as their pain may be, do not resolve to take medications and refuse them all. There are others who very rarely take the medication, and then only on conditions as to the way, quantity or quality. Finally there are others who swallow any type of medication given to them by the doctor. What do you say about these three types of infirm individuals? For certain, the first ones show that they do not care much about their health. The second ones care little. The last ones, they are sick in their body, yes, but are wise in their mind, since on their part they do not omit anything that might restore their health. Let us take a closer look. To which category of infirm individuals do we belong? Do we accept willingly the medicines of tribulation or do we refuse them flatly?...

---

[1] Sir 2:4-5

3. For the time being there is no doubt that in receiving a humiliation, especially if it comes from a vile servant or a rude petulant, we feel bad about it. Yet do we forget that the doctor orders the medications and then he has them given out by the druggist or the nurse, that is by a less noble individual? Likewise God orders the medication of suffering and has people inferior or hostile to us give them to us, so that the medication may become even more beneficial.

4. A medicine is always bitter, therefore you are never forbidden to complain about it. The only thing you are asked is not to spill it or not take it. Humiliations are hard to swallow. Physical pains and spiritual afflictions are felt sharply, yet are they less meritorious if we bear with them with resignation? Jesus suffered in the garden as well as on Calvary. The martyrs suffered in their torments. They suffered, but did not give in and so they became saints. To suffer is human, to despair is of the damned.

5. Above all, let us see to it that we remain strong when given the medicines of dishonor and insult, since they are the most bitter ones. To employ all of one's abilities to do good to others and then be moked for it, to spend time and money to relieve human misfortunes and then receive bloody insults for it, how deep it hurts you! Yet even then, more than before, let us focus on God who sends his tribulations to us in this manner. Let us focus our attention on the wounds of our soul that, deep as they might be, still need a very powerful medication.

6. A medicine is administered at times to find out if our inner organs are healthy. Why does the Lord administer his medicines to men here on earth?... To find out who is holy

and who is not. Now, how could God welcome into paradise the evil and the good with no distinction? First of all he wants to test them. Doesn't a king have the right to examine those who are going to become his pages or equerries? Who is going to deny the Lord of his right to use the probe, that is the fiery knife of the doctor, to find out the state of health in a body? It is necessary that God sends his tribulations. He who bears with them is blessed, for he is sure that he is sound in faith, strong in virtues, fit to be welcomed into the paradise of the saints.

7. Isn't it better for us to be vexed at least a little? Thus we will see who we are and how far our virtue goes. As long as we experience tenderness in our devotions and good feelings in our holy resolutions, we cannot really trust ourselves. Don't you see how easy it is for us to talk more than to act? Don't you realize how oftentimes the wise themselves laugh at the wordiness of their discourses?

A Roman soldier, to prove his firm determination to fight for his country, lit a fire, placed his hand on it and held it there until the burns began to drip the fat. He was comforted all along by saying: "As I can bear with this torment, so I will bear the hardship of the battle.." Proofs are required of us, too. The best proof of health and vigour we can give is the suffering with great resignation. Did you understand, then, how advantageous suffering is? Have we all learned that the bitter cup of suffering can be a beneficial medicine for our passions?... May heaven be pleased if we know how to take advange of it.

REFLECTIONS

1. A beneficial medicine.
2. The evil of our passions.
3. It is cured with the remedy of tribulation.
4. There is nothing wrong feeling the pain in tribulation, yet it is ruinous to despair in experiencing it.
5. Let us most of all have patience in the trials of dishonor and insult.
6. There one proves whether he is just or not.
7. Let us, then, welcome any sort of tribulations, because a certain amount of suffering constitutes a wholesome remedy.

GOSPEL OF THE SEVENTH SUNDAY AFTER PENTECOST

Do you believe?

1. Our adversaries, the enemies of faith and Christian morals, make us a most bitter reproach. In the bitterness of their heart they say: "Do you believe? If you believed in God you would not seek your own interest. If you believed that after this life there is hell or heaven, you would strive to avoid the torment and merit the reward. You would see to it that everyone else would follow your example." Most bitter discourse! Do you think that today's Catholics deserve such a reproach?... Not all of them, but some do. Let us see to what degree they deserve the reproach of the impious.

The divine Savior says in today's Gospel: "Be on your guard against false prophets, who come to you in sheep's clothing but underneath are wolves on the prowl. You will know them from their deeds. Do you ever pick grapes from thornbushes, or figs from prickly plants? Never! Any sound tree bears good fruit, while a decayed tree bears bad fruit. A sound tree cannot bear bad fruit any more than a decayed tree can bear good fruit. Every tree that does not bear good fruit is cut down and thrown into the fire. You can tell a tree by its fruit. None of those who cry out, 'Lord, Lord,' will enter the kingdom of God but only the one who does the will of my Father in heaven."[1]

---

[1] Mt 7:15-21

Considering the sense of the discourse in the Gospel I ask myself in terror: what kind of a Christian am I?... Do I seek in everything the glory of my heavenly Father, or do I seek my glory also?... And terrified I question you, too: do you believe? "Now how can you claim that you believe - St. John himself is asking this question - you who give glory to one another, you who do not seek the glory that only comes from God?"[1] Let us focus our attention on answering this threatening question.

2. Ambitious individuals can be found even among Christians, who look for nothing but their own glory. They do nothing but speak of themselves when they set to work on an undertaking of good. In carrying it out they brag about their great abilities. In closing up their undertaking they stand their ground like a golden statue to see that everyone applauds them. What is this?

I dare to ask them: do you believe in God? Do you believe that the will and power to conduct a good undertaking come from God?... So, if you believe, how can you idolize yourselves in this way? It means that you do not believe. Too weakly you believe that there will be an after-life, because you think too much of this present life. You do not believe with a lively faith in God, because you do not serve him and do not love him as he deserves. What are you looking for, after all? You seek your own interest and glory! Now is anyone going to claim that a son who seeks nothing but his own satisfaction and not the satisfaction of his father, is a good son? Say it openly that he is an evil son. He acts as if in his father's house he is the only one who can stay, the proud

---

[1] Jn 5:44

and arrogant son. My brothers and sisters, let us be terrified in having to answer this first question.

3. What can diminish to a great degree or even deprive us of faith is the longing for the vain esteem of men. How simple-minded we are, how simple-minded! Do men have the ability to judge who we really are?... God is the only one who sees us in our hearts. If men attempt to judge us, are they going to exert themselves to examine our intentions and deeds? Given that they do that, who is going to assure us that those who bless us today are not going to curse us tomorrow?... The minds of men are so unstable, as so misleading are their hearts!

What matters to you, then, if others have a great esteem of you?... Don't even bother with it, don't bother at all. If praise is openly given to you, turn it down modestly. Care for God's praise. If the Lord praises you, what matters to you whether men praise you or reprove you?

4. However, you may be individuals who while seeking the glory of God, care even more for the glory of men. Yet, after all, who are these men in comparison with God? Are they at least like a bunch of laborers in comparison with many kings? They are much less, for all men together in the sight of God are as nothing.

So, you care so much that four wretched little fellows here on earth have esteem for you? Isn't it much better that the angels praise you, who are more numerous in number and much more glorious? Isn't it better that the apostles and martyrs, the virgins and the confessors praise you? Isn't better that the Blessed Virgin praises you? And if God himself comes to meet you and in the sight of the heavenly court fills you with his blessings, isn't this much better? You might say that the glory that comes from men you can see and feel, while the one that comes from God is concealed. So what? If it is concealed, isn't it more secure, much more abundant? How foolish we are, if while we set aside all longing for worldly praise we do not more closely cling to the glory that comes from God.

5. Give special attention at this point to recognize the more special value of the glory that is found in serving God. Raise your eyes on high. What do the blessed do? They praise God and in turn they are blessed by God. Those happy souls who see God are happy to be able to praise God and are applauded by God.

What about the just who on earth have a pure heart and always and in everything seek only the glory of the Lord, what kind of just are they?... They are so as to precisely resemble the saints in paradise. So, even here on earth, when a Christian seeks nothing but the esteem from God, then among the elect faithful to God that holy union and trust of heart and desires is established that is the pledge and beginning of the true blessedness that exists among the saints in paradise.

6. At this point I want to give you an example. I want to talk to you about St. Ignatius. He was a valiant captain in the army, longing for worldly glory. Yet, by divine assistance he reformed himself. At that point he set this maxim in his heart: everything for the greater glory of God. And he stuck to it. He benefited so much from it that he kept his faith in his heart always alive. He often said: "If everyone abandons the cross of the Savior, I will cling to it more tightly." He also nourished such a warm faith in his heart that he could say: "One thing only I seek: the Lord's glory For this I would like

to be able to save all the souls in the world. For God's glory I would like to dwell in deprivations and agonies till the end of the world. Oh, that I might lay across the gate of hell to prevent anyone else from falling into it and from cursing God for all eternity!"

Thus, for the glory of God, he longed that everyone considered him a madman. In his life he chose a life-style of holiness that is more common and less ostentatious. Dying, he pleaded with his confreres that, in burying him, they would throw his body away as a dead dog.

My brothers and sisters, let us choose St. Ignatius as our special advocate in knocking down the glory of the world. God himself, willing to give a special protector for this purpose to St. Maria Magdalene De' Pazzi, chose St. Ignatius. St. Maria Magdalene entrusted herself to him and set herself out on her way to perfection so well as you well know. Now I repeat to you again the question: do you believe?... If you believe, renounce at last the glory of men and seek only the glory that comes from God.

REFLECTIONS

1. Do you believe?
2. Ambition makes one lose his faith.
3. What is, after all, the esteem of men? And the esteem of God, how valuable is it?...
4. Let us renounce completely the desire for worldly esteem.
5. The just man, who esteems only the glory of God, deserves what makes him resemble the blessed in paradise.
6. Be comforted by the example of St. Ignatius.

GOSPEL OF THE EIGHTH SUNDAY AFTER PENTECOST

He who holds out to the end is victorious

1. It is a most useful maxim at all times and is very appropriate in our times. The maxim is as follows: he who holds out to the end is victorious. Oh, I wish Christians would understand this and put it into action at the civil and religious level! We Italians, above all, would not be covered by such a shame coming to us from everywhere.

He who endures is victorious. The evil ones win, though they are siding wrongdoing. How can good people not win since they are in the part of what is just? Let us listen to what the holy Gospel tells us.

Jesus said to his disciples: "A rich man had a manager who was reported to him for dissipating his property. He summoned him and said, 'What is this I hear about you? Give me an account of your service, for it is about to come to an end.' The manager thought to himself, 'What shall I do next? My employer is sure to dismiss me. I cannot dig ditches. I am ashamed to go begging. I have it! Here is a way to make sure that people will take me into their homes when I am let go.' So he called in each of his master's debtors, and said to the first, 'How much do you owe my master?' The man replied, 'A hundred jars of oil.' The manager said, 'Take your invoice, sit down quickly, and make it fifty.' Then he said to a second, 'How much do you owe?' The answer came, 'A hundred measures of wheat,' and the manager said, 'Take your invoice and make it eighty.' The owner then gave his devious employee credit for being enterprising! Why? Because the worldly take more initiative than the other-worldly when it comes to dealing with their own kind. What I say to you is this: Make friends for yourselves through your use of this world's goods, so that when they fail you, a lasting reception will be yours.[1]

Did you get the lesson? Isn't it true that the evil ones win over their iniquitous projects? How come that a good Christian remains idle? It is time to dispel idleness, and let us act! He who holds out to the end is victorious. Let us prove this maxim, because if heaven blesses us with understanding it, it will certainly benefit our soul. The Apostle Paul suggests: "Do not be conquered by evil but conquer evil with good."[2]

2. The Apostle, then, says: "Do not be conquered by evil, but conquer evil with good." To make you understand this maxim I am going to give you an example. Elzeario had just received the inheritance of his father, the prince of Naples, and was going through the most confidential papers of his beloved father. What does he find out?

He learns that a courtier, reputed most faithful, very animatedly and up to the last moment tried to convince his father to disinherit his son Elzeario. How quickly he felt his blood run to his head! Yet he immediately thought: "How miserable am I if I let myself be run by anger!" At that moment the courtier, that evil fellow, comes in. The poor Elzeario felt his blood run cold again! Yet he thought: "I do not intend to alienate this man more, but I want to make of

---

[1] Lk 16:1-9
[2] Rm 12:21

him a friend of mine; I don't want to be won over by his wickedness, but by my benevolence I want to remove his wickedness." He exerted himself so much and so charitably that at the end he achieved a most noble victory.

It resembles the victory which the divine Savior obtained on the cross. They all cursed and blasphemed him, while he was praying for all so fervently. This caused the reaction that while he was dying people left Calvary striking their chests repentantly. In this sense a Christian who endures will be victorious. Or, if he cannot obtain the complete conversion of his adversary, at least he will give him a good example, doing nothing wrong himself, but much good by praying and wishing all prosperity to his adversary.

3. He who holds out to the end wins even over the devil and his ministers. The devil, who is he after all?... He is like a furious dog, kept in chains by God where he belongs. When the devil tempts you, don't get close to him. Spit on his face from afar and you will win quickly. This is what St. Anthony did in the desert when Satan appeared to him under the appearance of horrible individuals or ferocious tigers during the night. Furthermore, when Satan tempts you, increase the number of your good deeds, mortifications and prayer. This is what St. Anthony did and what did he not obtain? The heavens opened up over his head, and he heard the voice of the Lord who said: "You have fought a valiant fight, Anthony!" He who holds out to the end will be victorious. It doesn't take much effort. Every Christian, if he wills, can defeat Satan.

Furthermore, as he can trample underfoot the prince of evil, so he can subdue his ministers. When a blasphemer incites you to curse, is it too hard for you to resist him and instead to persuade him to stop. This is what St. Jerome

Emiliani did on his way to Somasca. When someone rouses your sensuality, why don't you yell at him to correct him? Thus Pafnutius won over and converted the most evil Taides, who from being an evil seducer became a saint. When someone else tries to take you away from piety, exert yourselves in leading him to church and the Sacraments. Thus St. Bernard convinced his brothers to enter religious life, while they had come to take him away from it. Most noble victories! Isn't it true that they are very many? And you can reap them all! Isn't it better then to hold out to the end to be victorious through perseverance?

4. He who holds out to the end will be victorious. Finally we can obtain a victory that is certainly the noblest one. We can be victorious over our own passions. Especially the passions of the senses wage harder battles and attempt to subdue our reason and conscience. Yet let us step on this vile flesh of ours. Let us mortify the senses of our body, let us mortify the faculties of our mind. Let us restrain our heart so as not to lose it. Do we need to travel far away in order to assault our enemies? We have them within ourselves.

St. Francis of Assisi, moved by passions, threw himself into rose-bushes in the middle of January and immediately the thorned bushes bloomed with most beautiful roses. St. Thomas Aquinas resorted to red hot coals to put to flight a seducer once for all. He who holds out to the end is victorious. Apply this maxim to the many more cases both in private as well as public life, above all in matters of religion. You will always find that he who holds out to the end is victorious.

Let us be strong, brothers and sisters, and let us break at last those chains of slavery that entangle us. They are so many and have entangled us for so long because we, fearful, have allowed ourselves to be caught, and because we, vile, have lingered in idleness. Away with the chains of slavery. Let us set ourselves in the bright day of Catholic freedom. Forward, forward! He who holds out to the end will be victorious.

REFLECTIONS

1. He who hold out to the end will be victorious.
2. An adversary is defeated by counteracting his fierce hatred with gentleness.
3. The devil is won over by spitting on his face, and his ministers by leading them to repentance.
4. We win over our own passions by subduing them always to reason. He who holds out to the end will be victorious in re-establishing everywhere the religious order that was perturbed.

GOSPEL OF THE NINTH SUNDAY
AFTER PENTECOST

That flesh be put to death!

1. There are today Christians who have become so cruel in their hearts or so fickle in their minds that frantically cry out: "Death! Death!" Lacking courage to say it in the light of the day, they vilely write it in the darkness of the night: "Death! Death!", and then they wish death for one person or even for an entire category of individuals. Viles! Viles! Shout it for something. Do you know who should be wished death instead? Nothing else but your own flesh and passions. Shout it with all your heart: "Let the flesh be put to death, yes let flesh be put to death!", for by putting the flesh to death you will give life to the spirit.

It is very true, and St. Paul makes us sure of it. Writing to his fellow Romans he says: "If you live according to the flesh, you will die; but if by the spirit you put to death the evil deeds of the body, you will live."[1] Unfortunate citizens of Jerusalem, who did not know how to live by the spirit, and instead succombed to the flesh in everything! Behold what happened to them as a consequence. Threats and lightnings as we read in the holy Gospel.

Coming within the sight of the city of Jerusalem, Jesus Christ wept over it and said: "'If only you had known the path of peace this day; but you have completely lost it from view! Days will come upon you when your enemies encircle you with a rampart, hem you in, and press you hard from every

---

[1] Rm 8:13

side. They will wipe you out, you and your children within your walls, and leave not a stone on a stone within you, because you failed to recognize the time of your visitation.' Then he entered the temple and began ejecting the traders saying: Scripture has it, 'My house is meant for a house of prayer' but you have made it 'a den of thieves.' He was teaching in the temple area from day to day."[1]

This is the threat of lightnings of the divine Savior. The lightnings, then, came as you well know. How much did they hurt the miserable ones for not having cried out: "Punishment and death to our flesh!" If they had done so, they would certainly have been saved.

2. Let us consider a little what is the body with his passions, and what is the soul with her virtues. A body with his passions is a monument of mire, trying to vomit in order to get rid of the soul. The spirit, instead, with her virtues of grace and charity, is a monument of virtue inhabited by God as in a temple, and in which the heart of Jesus Christ our Savior rejoices as on his throne. Which one do you like most? A monument of mire or a sacred monument?...

Do not destroy the monument of mire because it does not belong to you, for God gave it to you. Sustain it as needed so as not to collapse, yet do not devote too much care for it. Beautify more and more the monument of the soul, for it is the dwelling of the Most High. Yet pay much attention to what is suggested by St. Paul: "If you live according to the flesh, you will kill the spirit." The house of the soul is built and embellished by allowing the building of the body to be exposed to the winds and slashed by the storms. The external body is the servant of the soul, it is the container of the soul,

---

[1] Lk 19:41-47

as well as the jail of the soul. What care should we have for such a vile servant, for a fragile vase, for the cell of a jail that is going to be left behind as soon as possible?

3. Miserable we are if we live according to the flesh! Miserable both here in this life as well as in the next to come. Let the body have all its pleasures. You will soon be approached by three horrible figures who will attack you one by one and then all together. Take off, take off or you will be dead.

The first horrible beast is the beast of mortal sin. By satisfying the flesh fully in its cravings, you fall from the state of grace, and ask Satan to enter your heart. Miserable ones, you are done! All the while you feel in your heart a guilt that gives you no peace. In your mind you feel a pain that makes you feverish. In your body you see sores that soon become cancerous. Miserable ones, you are dead even in your body! And if you die with a mortal sin in your soul, you are even dead for hell. Be at least terrified by the figure of a thousand devils and beneficially touched by the sight of the terrors of hell. Miserable are we if in order to please the flesh we damn our soul! Let the flesh be put to death! Let the flesh be put to death so that the spirit may live.

4. How fortunate we are if the spirit lives! We are immediately welcomed by the blessed angels to crown us. The angel of life comes and keeps away from us the ailments of evil. The venerable figures of the patriarchs and the prophets, who were so moderate in responding to the demands of the flesh, lived for centuries looking back at their past years spent in prosperity and success. Likewise in Christianity, those who conduct an apostolic life, satisfied with what is strictly necessary to live and be clothed with,

these, too, come to us in their noble figure of long-lived personages!

When the soul is healthy, she gains a continuous growth of grace. The lucky one day by day sees the treasure of her merits multiply. At every moment she experiences in her heart the joy of the life of God, that looks like flowing in the veins to cheer the life of the heart. What ineffable sweetness! How lovely is a just and holy life!

Finally, the life of grace is taken over by the life of glory. This takes place in paradise, as soon as the soul, upon leaving her faithful companion, the body, flies to the enjoyment in heaven. Admire the souls of the saints in paradise, and then come to acknowledge that it is proper to exclaim with all affection: "Put the flesh to death so that the spirit may live!"

5. I wish that heaven would allow us to conduct here on earth the angelic life the blessed already enjoy in heaven! This, however, is not possible on earth. It is enough that we live a spiritual life, that is a mortified life. Let us distance ourselves from the flesh in all its pleasures, for this is beastly. Let us satisfy the flesh within the limits assigned to it by reason by a common and moderate life, which fits a Christian. If we add to it special mortifications as supplementary, then the life of this Christian becomes spiritual. In this sense, fortunate is he who mortifies his flesh to let the spirit triumph.

In this exercise of mortification wise Christians never say it is enough. They mortify the cravings of the heart. They mortify the senses of the body. They do not allow the flesh to have any satisfaction, and so they restrain it as much as possible. Blessed mortification, that originates so much good as we have seen above! Mortification for the flesh! Death for the cravings of the flesh so that the spirit may enjoy his life.

REFLECTIONS

1. Let the flesh be put to death!
2. One or the other: he who cares only for the flesh causes the death of the soul.
3. He who lives according to the flesh has to deal with three figures of death.
4. He, then, who lives according to the spirit, embraces three angels of life.
5. Why don't all people live according to the spirit?

GOSPEL OF THE TENTH SUNDAY AFTER PENTECOST

Is the Lord the servant of men?

1. The children of man are wretched in mind and evil in their heart! They take advantage of their gifts from the Lord to give vent to their whims. They ask God for talents, from God they expect glory and honor, and once they have received them they enjoy themselves in dissolving themselves in any sort of worldly pleasures, if not in any kind of blatantly manifest sin. What is this? Why, while God fills you with good, do you insult him more arrogantly? So, God is the servant of your whims? There are Christians who attempt to adjust the Most High to themselves. Listen to the parable of the Pharisee and the tax collector and you will see if this is not so. We read from St. Luke.

"Jesus then spoke this parable addressed to those who believed in their own self-righteousness while holding everyone else in contempt: Two men went up to the temple to pray; one was a Pharisee, the other a tax collector. The Pharisee with head unbowed prayed in this fashion; 'I give you thanks, O God, that I am not like the rest of men - grasping, crooked, adulterous - or even like this tax collector. I fast twice a week. I pay tithes on all I possess.' The other man, however, kept his distance, not even daring to raise his eyes to heaven. All he did was beat his breast and say, 'O God, be merciful to me, a sinner.' Believe me, this man went home from the temple justified but the other did not. For everyone who exalts himself shall be humbled while he who humbles himself shall be exalted."[1]

Who would say that the Pharisee, gifted so much by God, would speak to praise himself so strangely and with such a detriment for the reputation of his neighbor?... Yet he is not alone. He has companions among the Christians. The Lord feels very bad about it. Through the prophet Isaiah the Lord expresses his sadness as follows: "You burdened me with your sins, and wearied me with your crimes."[2] Can a thing more iniquitous than this be done? Hearts of Christians, listen to this and make a resolution.

2. There was a time when the Son of God came to earth to serve men. On this earth on which we step men gazed at the face of the Redeemer. Then a cry of wonder resounded in heaven as well as on earth that said: "God loved the world so much that he gave his only Son."[3] Saying so, they could say no more, astonished dumb-striken with amazement.

The holy prophets, who thousands of years before saw in spirit the ordeal of sweat, suffering and agony which the Savior was going to undergo, were desolate and could not believe it. Heaven! What would those holy personages say now in seeing how, after Jesus humbled himself to death on the cross two thousand years ago, men and even Christians act with such wickedness?

It is an abuse for people to expect that God be their servant so that they may give vent to their whims of sin! Yet such ungratefulness does take place. God, in his goodness, bestows riches, gives talents, gives strength to our body. God bestows the gift of sacred knowledge, plenty of Sacraments

---

[1] Lk 18:9-14
[2] Is43:24
[3] Jn 3:16

and grace. Yet how do men avail themselves of all this? They employ their God-given abilities to sin. Unfortunately they even make use of the gifts of grace to sin more ungratefully. Spare me from being more specific, for I hate it too much.

3. Nevertheless realize how far the Lord goes in sustaining especially some sinners. He bears with habitual sinners. Good God! The Lord, the Most High, sustains them in good health so that they may do good, instead they commit every sort of iniquity! The Lord defers punishing them as he could do, and they have the temerity to sin even more wantonly. The Lord stretches his hand to spare them from the devils so that they may not be swallowed up by them, and they multiply their excesses and do not even for a moment think: "I have sinned, O Lord!"

If any servant of yours did to you half of the abuses which certain sinners do against God, you certainly would cry out to defend the honor of your person! Nonetheless, God remains silent, and since he remains silent, the sinners keep on committing their iniquities, spending their days in idleness and offending God, who benefits them so abundantly.

4. What a monstrosity this is! Emperor Basil used to hunt for fun. Once he was attacked by a deer that kept on tossing him with its antlers. A farmer rushed to save him. For this happy event everyone expected that the fortunate farmer would be rewarded handsomely. Basil, instead, once back to his palace, said: "Did you not know that? It was that evil farmer that put me in danger... I command that he be immediately hung!"... Wretched one! Very soon the man whom everyone expected to be honored with the applause of the entire population, was dying hanging on the gibbet. This

179

fact is reported as an excess of ungratefulness and excessive infamy.

Yet it takes place oftentimes among men. We hunt for amusements, which often are dangerous or manifestly dishonest, and all the while we let ourselves be tossed by the antlers of so many devils of hell. Jesus Christ, the merciful savior, comes and gives his hand to protect us from the harm of the elements or of the spirits of hell. Finding ourselves safe, we say: "It is not God who saved us." We claim that we saved ourselves and we even brag about it by adding, more ungrateful than the Jews themselves: "Crucify Jesus! Crucify Jesus!" As a matter of fact we push him up to the top of that mountain to die.

Oh, my brothers and sisters, have pity for Jesus who is dying! Have pity for the Savior who delivers us from death! If he knew that it would be for our benefit, the Savior would even fall before us to plead with us. Didn't he plead already on the cross? Do we still need so much that God may spare us from such a shame? That's enough, that's enough. It is too much that we have made God serve us in our sins so cruelly in the past. It is too much that we have oppressed him by imposing on him the burden of so many iniquities which by now have become a habit for us. That's enough. It is an outrageous affront that man may so horribly abuse the goodness of the Lord.

REFLECTIONS

1. Is the Lord the servant of men?
2. Jesus Christ has already acted as a servant in the high mystery of his divine incarnation.
3. Yet sinners, and among these those who have the habit of sinning, really exhaust the patience of the divine Savior.
4. How long will such a monstrosity continue among men?

GOSPEL OF THE ELEVENTH SUNDAY AFTER PENTECOST

A son of the devil

1. Once a philosopher was asked: "Of all creatures which one is the most monstrous?" The wise man answered: "The corrupted man is the one." A young man approached the famous Jesuit Francois Oudin and said to him: "I am an atheist, I do not believe in God." Father Oudin stood and kept looking the young man up and down without saying a word, but only showing signs of great marvel. "What are you looking at so intently?" "I look at the animal who calls himself an atheist, for this is the first one I have ever seen."

I check with the sacred Gospel and ask myself: a Christian sinner, who is he? Faith gives me the answer: he is the son of the devil. A stupid son, who cannot understand, cannot speak, who is tormented by Satan, like the deaf-mute of whom we read today in the Gospel. Listen to the text.

"Jesus left the Tyrian territory and returned by the way of Sidon to the Sea of Galilee, into the district of the Ten Cities. Some people brought him a deaf man who had a speech impediment and begged him to lay his hands on him. Jesus took him off by himself away from the crowd. He put his finger into the man's ears and, spitting, touched his tongue; then he looked up to heaven and emitted a groan. He said to him, 'Ephphatha!' (that is, 'Be opened!') At once the man's ears were opened; he was freed from the impediment, and began to speak plainly. Then Jesus enjoined them strictly not to tell anyone; but the more he ordered them not to, the more they proclaimed it. Their amazement went beyond all bounds: 'He has done evrything well! He makes the deaf hear and the mute speak!'"[1]

A deaf man who cannot hear is the image of the sinner who closes his ears so as not to hear the orders of the Lord. A mute who does not open his mouth is the symbol of the wicked man who does not want to speak to acknowledge his God. Poor sinner! Do you disdain to acknowledge that you are the son of the Lord?... Whose son are you, then? There is no doubt. The sinner is the son of the devil. Listen to what St. John the Apostle writes: "The father you spring from is the devil, and willingly you carry out his wishes."[2] Let us reflect on this horrible paternity, so that a sinner, perhaps, horrified, may come back to invoke the Lord of heaven.

2. One can claim to be the son of someone on four different accounts: by nature, by adoption, by doctrine, and by imitation. I will explain more specifically. Children by nature are those generated by their biological father. In this sense no one can be a son of the devil. In another case, a respected man takes a child abandoned on the street and adopts him. This is referred to as having children by adoption. Not even in this sense can the devil claim sinners as his children. Someone, however, can consider himself a son of someone, for being instructed and educated by him. Unfortunately in this sense the devil is the father of all those who follow his maxims. Furthermore, someone can consider himself a son of a man because he imitates his ways in speaking and in acting. In this sense, too, horrible to say yet very true, sinners are children of the devil by imitation.

---

[1] Mk 7:31-37
[2] Jn 8:44

Sinners who show yourselves to be so bold, boast of that, of being children of the devil. You act as gods here on earth. Do you expect that everyone bows at your coming? You are children of such an ugly father! Is it possible that you are not horrified by being told that you are children of the devil?

3. Truly the wretched sinners are children of the devil, because they seek nothing but to resemble him. They have no limits in their ambition. In heaping up riches they always say: "Thousands upon thousands, millions upon millions." In venting their dishonesties or debaucheries or jealousies or revenges, do you think that they set a limit? They keep shouting: *"Affer, affer (Give, give)"*[1], and in eating and having fun they are insatiable. What else should they do in order to resemble Satan more closely? They would do more if their energies were greater. Yet, whatever they cannot achieve by their abilities, they grasp it by desire. Thus they keep going on, longing for vengeance, lust, seduction, and most shameful deception.

They, indeed, do much more than even Satan does. Lucifer chafes with anger, but is tied with chains. Sinners, instead, show themselves under the appearance of upright personages and make their way even into the most guarded sheepfolds. They enter the cloisters, the churches, the most religious Christian families, and sneek into them a dangerous book, a mundane leaflet, an alluring picture. Then they keep it up with licentious discourses, and then with friendly and intimate behaviors that lead to ruinous falls. Would Satan have himself involved in that filthy matter, since he is a spirit, though evil? He has found ministers for himself in scandalous

---

[1] Pr 30:15

184

sinners, habitual blasphemers, and rapacious gluttons. The devil makes use of these, and these indeed do much more that Satan himself would accomplish.

What a ruin the apostates and herestics of the past centuries have caused! How many are sent to perdition today by those most wretched individuals who seem to live just to cause the dissolution of the Church of Jesus Christ! They are truly children of the devil. True demons with flesh and bones, against whom time will be set aside to pour the anger of the Lord.

4. Let us think of what is going to happen at the end of the world. Then the children of the devil will be uncovered, those who now walk on earth as gods. They will be seen then! What a terror finding himself in the claws of Lucifer, that is of a traitor, a rebel, a criminal, guilty of hurting His Majesty! Then they will see their guilt, yet it will be too late for them for making any reparation.

They will shudder to see the happiness that surrounds the children of God. These, who have lived on earth in abandonment or contempt, will then appear in all the glory of the children adopted by God. They will appear in the splendor as they rightly deserve, children who have conducted themselves according to the maxims of the heavenly Father, whose virtues of perfection and holiness they imitated as much as they were able to.

What do you say, my brothers and sisters? Do you think that great will be the glory and happiness that will surround you?... Take courage, then, and be more and more dear children of the Lord. Have pity in the recesses of your heart for the children of the devil. What a pity for an individual who, being able to be a child of God, chooses to be the child of Satan instead!

REFLECTIONS

1. The children of the devil.
2. By two unfortunate accounts sinners are the wretched children of the devil.
3. They are children and ministers of Satan, involved in undertakings of ruin.
4. It will be seen one day.

GOSPEL OF THE TWELFTH SUNDAY
AFTER PENTECOST

Christian fortune

1. People of our time love running after the chances of fortune, yet they are never able to grasp it. What is fortune?... Seek it, yet you will never be able to find it in any place here on earth. Fortune cannot be found here. To grasp it, one must rise above the stars and find it in paradise. Once you find it, you will call it 'Christian fortune', since fortune cannot be found other than in what comes from Jesus Christ. Do you wish to have this fortune dwell in your house? Ask for it, and kindly it will come to you.

St. Paul writes to the Romans: "We know that God makes all things work together for the good of those who have been called according to his decree."[1] The discourse of today's holy Gospel hints at this very same thing.

"Jesus said to his disciples: Blest are the eyes that see what you see. I tell you, many prophets and kings wished to see what you see but did not see it, and to hear what you hear but did not hear it.

On one occasion a lawyer stood up to pose to him this problem: 'Teacher, what must I do to inherit everlasting life?' Jesus answered him: 'What is written in the law? How do you read it?' He replied: 'You shall love the Lord your God with all your heart, with all your soul, with all your strength, and with all your mind; and your neighbor as yourself.' Jesus

---

[1] Rm 8:28

said, 'You have answered correctly. Do this and you shall live.'"[1]

Did you understand, my brothers and sisters?... Love God and you shall live. This is Christian fortune. Those who work and do so with the pious intention of pleasing God, obtain that every undertaking of theirs comes to good. This is your fortune, brothers and sisters. Let us take a closer look at it.

2. Think of a family with numerous children, who obey faithfully their good father and work diligently and untiringly. That family cannot but prosper, for everyone contributes to their success. Oh, that Christians, children of the heavenly Father, would strive with equal attention to obey God and work in the field entrusted to them by Divine Providence! Prosperity would easily come by in our towns as well, and our entire country would become flourishing.

At least let us take care of ourselves in particular. Let us love the Lord. He who operates in everything to please the Most High, truly will be blessed by God. Isn't it an ineffable consolation for our heart? As long as one operates with the pious intention, whatever he does he puts it forward as a treasure for the glory of paradise. God does not leave without its recompense a pious thought, a dear affection, or a caring step. It is claimed in the holy Gospel that God will give paradise to whoever gives a glass of water to the least one for God's sake. How much more will He give us if, acting with pious intention, we will offer to the Lord all our strengths and all the acts of our lives?

---

[1] Lk 10:23-28

3. Think of a good son in the house of his father. If he is healthy and enterprising in whatever he does, he has good reasons for rejoicing for it with his father. If attacked by an adversary, he goes to his father for defense. If hurt when at grips with his attacker, he cries out for help and son and father stick together even more.

All the events of life here below can be reduced to two categories, some good and some bad. Yet the just man can equally profit from both. For whatever good happens to him, the just praises the Lord and goes to his presence with gratefulness. If something bad happens to him, as in cases of annoyances from people, he bears with them with great patience and all along he exercises many virtues of charity, meekness and other similar ones. If evil comes from the devil's temptations, a good Christian makes use of them to entrust himself more readily to the Lord, to detach himself from earthly things. If the just man happens to commit the evil of a sin, and immediately regrets it, he humbles himself for it. He entrusts himself quickly and with greater affection to the Lord, thus more solicitously he obtains to adhere to God and that the Lord adhere to him. Isn't this an utmost fortune for a Christian?... Can anyone else be found who, as a Christian does, is able to have converted into good even that evil which would cause great condemnation for others who are wicked?

4. Let us go back to the children of that numerous family. Some of them are obedient to their father and act with the full intent of pleasing him, sparing no pains in doing so. The father foresees that these children of his will always do good. The other children, instead, despise being under their father, and so they do not work at all or they do so at whim. The father foresees that evil will fall upon these. Nonthelesse

it is each individual who causes good or evil by his own action. Therefore, good Christians, be diligent in doing everything uprightly. Double your work to obtain that God crowns you. The Lord gives you his help, while you bring to it the work of your hands and the attention of your mind.

5. You might argue that if God has already established who will be saved, you cannot understand how those who are referred to as reprobates can escape damnation. Did I not tell you to love God and then wait for him to take you into paradise? Why do you want to search into predestination and grace, which are profound mysteries even for the scholars? Proceed with simplicity and think this way in your heart: "He who does good will be saved, he who does evil will be damned." Are you not satisfied with this reason, which is so apparent for everyone?...

In our account, let us avail ourselves of our very own ignorance to glorify God. Doesn't the son of a king, though wretched, enjoy looking at the majesty, wisdom, and power of his father, even though he is unable to comprehend its full extent?... Thus let us rejoice even more that God is immense, and we are poor and wretched creatures who barely can look at the splendor of the sun. This, too, is a fortune that satisfies our reason and pleases the soul. Blessed be the Lord, who has sown the seed of an adventurous fortune in the hearts of his faithful Christians.

REFLECTIONS

1. Christian fortune.
2. A son who acts with a good intent obtains fortune.
3. Every event in his life ends up being advantageous for him.
4. Yet he must strive for it.
5. For he who does good will be saved, while he who does evil will be condemned.

GOSPEL OF THE THIRTEENTH SUNDAY AFTER PENTECOST

Walk in the daylight

1. Pilgrims in this valley of tears, we have to undergo a very, very long journey from earth to heaven, a disastrous journey, because it has been given as a penance to those who have sinned. It is a fatiguing journey, because it is filled with dangers from above, and because lions from hell hide in the thickets. Miserable is the traveler, if being able to undertake his journey in daylight, decides to do it in the dark of the night!

In the holy Gospel of today we find wretched travelers who, perhaps because of traveling through a place and at a time which were not proper, ended up by being caught up with a miserable calamity, leprosy. They had to stay there and wail until the time when they heard that the divine Savior was passing by. From a distance they cried out, "Jesus, Master, have pity on us!" Good for them that they pleaded with their heart. Jesus cured them and so he took them out of the darkness of night and set them back on their journey in the beautiful light of the day. To the leper who came back to thank him openly, Jesus said: "Stand up and go your way; your faith has been your salvation."[1]

My brothers and sisters, let us set out with zest in the daylight that brightens the way of the holy Gospel. We will achieve salvation. Let us follow the advice of St. Paul to the Romans when he says: "Let us live honorably as in daylight;

---

[1] Lk 17:11-19

not in carousing and drunkness, not in sexual excess and lust, not in quarreling and jealousy. Rather, put on the Lord Jesus Christ and make no provision for the desires of the flesh."[1] With these good dispositions we are expected to complete our journey from the earth to heaven. Let us take a look at the way more closely.

2. Contrast the joyfulness of the day of Christmas with the horror of a stormy night of paganism or heresy. In the serene day of a feast day we see people well educated and dressed up. They visit their families with love, gathering with one another on the streets, smiling sweetly to their friends on the way. They hasten to church with fervor and share with one another the embrace of peace in holy affection. Peace on earth, peace to men of good will; peace to those who journey in the splendor of the sun of Jesus Christ.

Here you are, my beloved Christians. Do you feel in your heart a great gratitude for God who has called you in the brightness of such a day? It was not so with so many of our pagan brothers and sisters of Asia or savages of Africa, as well as to so many others and heretics in the Americas or in Europe. Miserable, miserable! Oh, how staggering they go on their journey! How do they vacillate in their mind, how cruel they are in their heart, and how they resemble the drunkard in their walking. Hasten to save them, or they will all perish! Fortunate we are who journey in full daylight in blessing!

3. In the daylight of a beautiful and holy day good are the deeds which we do and prudent are the discourses we carry out. Let us think once again of the joy of Christmas Day. On that solemnity above all even the slightest idea of

---

[1] Rm 13:13-14

immoderate eating or drinking, or drowsiness is avoided. There is no sign of quarrel or contention or envy on that day. Good Christians are all intent on enjoying a holy day, conducting themselves soberly with each other, piously with God, justly with their neighbor.

What is the purpose of excesses and immodesties?... These are iniquities carried out by pagans in the darkness of the night. Contentions in order to take advantage of others, disputes of honor, envies for superiority are all iniquities brought forward by heretics and evil people to vent their passions. Yet they do not journey in the daylight, feeling their way in the darkness of the night. How do you feel about it? May heaven spare you from carrying out a gloomy deed of sin in the full daylight of Catholic faith.

4. Look there, Jesus Christ, the sun of justice, who shows the way to his people. How radiant he is in his face, how shining he is in his person, how sweet in his manners, and attractive in his look! It is impossible to look at Jesus and not be drawn to follow in his footsteps. Let us all, then, clothe ourselves with the splendor of Jesus Christ. Let us clothe ourselves with the wounds of his passion, with the blood of his sufferings. Let us lay our heart on the heart of Jesus. Listen to the heart beats of that divine heart, let us listen to his moanings, let us uncover his pious desires and see to it that our heart becomes sweet like Jesus' heart, meek and patient like his. Let us be Christians. What does it mean Christian?... *"Christianus alter Christus"*, says the holy Doctor. That's right. Isn't the son expected to imitate his father? Yet, how have we imitated Jesus Christ so far?... May heaven be pleased that we know how to imitate Christ now.

5. For this purpose let us mortify the desires of the flesh. It is the rebel that fights us so vehemently. The tyrant would like to subdue the spirit. It is not right that the cruel flesh is satisfied. As a servant let it obey to reason, which is the master par excellence.

What a beautiful example the divine Savior gave to us in this! The tender limbs of the Baby Jesus lay on the harsh hay, in the severe winter. His hand in the shop of Nazareth became callous under the exercise of continuous labor. During his ministry, he sweats from the morning until the evening, and at night he lays his head on a stone to take his brief rest. Think whether he is longing for excessive food or drink. He begged for a piece of bread and in his journeying through Palestine he contained his thirst so that he would not misstep for an instant in converting souls. When the hour of his death approached, he exposed his body to be scourged and finally he laid on the wood of the cross.

What do you say, Christians? Do you have anything to add? If you care for the love you have for your Redeemer who leads in such a bright way, do not spare the flesh its mortifications. Let us clothe ourselves with the virtues of our Lord Jesus Christ and along with him let us walk in the bright splendor of the doctrine until we attain paradise.

REFLECTIONS

1. Journey in the daylight.
2. The joyful day of Christianity.
3. In such a day everyone appears dressed with virtues.
4. Let us all follow Jesus Christ, the sun of justice.
5. Let us clothe ourselves with his virtues.

GOSPEL OF THE FOURTEENTH SUNDAY AFTER PENTECOST

Is our heart pure?

1. Here I am to pose a question for you. Tell me: is your heart pure? You have sinned and have repented, have sinned and have gone to confession. Now, is your heart pure? Let us find out, for this after all is a very important matter. If your heart is pure, then it will not be so attached to the things of earth any more.

The Lord says in the holy Gospel: "No man can serve two masters. He will either hate one and love the other or be attentive to one and despise the other. You cannot give yourself to God and money. I warn you, then: do not worry about your livelihood, what you are to eat or drink or use for clothing. Is not life more than food? Is not the body more valuable than clothes?... Look at the birds in the sky. They do not sow or reap, they gather nothing into barns; yet your heavenly Father feeds them. Are not you more important than they? Which of you by worrying can add a moment to his life-span? As for clothes, why be concerned? Learn a lesson from the way the wild flowers grow. They do not work; they do not spin. Yet I assure you, not even Solomon in all his splendor was arrayed like one of these. If God can clothe in such splendor the grass of the field, which blooms today and is thrown on the fire tomorrow, will he not provide much more for you, O weak in faith! Stop worrying, then, over questions like, 'What are we to eat, or what are we to drink, or what are we to wear?' The unbelievers are always running after these things. Your heavenly Father knows all that you need. Seek first the kingship over you, his way of holiness, and all these things will be given you besides."[1]

What is your heart telling you? Are you pure in your soul? Jeremiah writes: "Cleanse your heart of evil, O Jerusalem, that you may be saved. How long must your pernicious thoughts lodge within you?"[2] Let us give an answer to this serious question. Let us hasten to cleanse our heart and remove pernicious thoughts from it.

2. There are many good souls who commit many venial sins of vain pride, impatience, and distractions in their duties. They regret it and confess their sins, thereby cleansing their hearts. In so doing they clean their hearts for sure, yet they do not cleanse it fully. To have their hearts fully purified the souls have to detest their faults vehemently, abhoring them with great hate. They need to look at their slight sins with such a displeasure and horror which any offense that maliciously injures the Most High deserves.

Listen to the following example. St. Teresa, no doubt, confessed her sins here and then when she was a young lady. Her sins, truly, were only venial, yet they were many, as time wasted in vanities, fickleness in futile readings, capriciousness in ambition and the like. She confessed them and felt very bad about them, yet she was not able to abhor them as a truly faithful soul should. The Lord appeared to her, holding a white piece of cloth that was covered all over with very tiny black stains. St. Teresa was horrified and asked the Lord: "What is this?..." Jesus said: "This is an image of your soul and a sign for you that you will move from venial sins to

---

[1] Mt 6:24-33
[2] Jer 4:14

grave sins and you will be damned unless you take better care of your salvation." How she then began to detest the malice of her sins! Not only did she cleanse her heart, but she cleansed it so as to make it completely spotless.

3. Is your heart pure? See to it that not only thoughts that are sinful, which would be a tragedy, but even thoughts that are dangerous do not feel at home in it. Do you hold attachment to riches, comforts, self esteem? Do you seek worldly entertainments and conversations? It's a sign that your heart is clean, since there is no mortal sin in it, yet it is not pure, since it is not free from earthly affections. As long as thoughts come and go and come back again, yet you detest them, there is nothing wrong with it. What is wrong is when you let them feel at home in your heart.

Imagine that you have been entrusted with the care of a jar filled with purest honey. Flies and mosquitos come and go, leave and come back, yet they are very angry because they cannot get their proboscis into the vase. Yet if you open the vase only for an instant, the insects get into the vase eagerly and your honey would be spoiled.

The vase is your mind. Keep the sense of sight well guarded. Guard the senses of speech and hearing. The thoughts, not finding a way to get in, will leave. If they come back, they have to leave again more frustrated than before. Souls of the just, is, then, your heart pure?... Question your conscience. If it tells you that you have no affection for harmful thoughts, then your heart must be pure.

4. If nothing else, will it be enough that your regret for your faults is only slight to have your heart pure? Not at all, your regret must be very great. Divert your heart completely from earthly vanities.

The Hebrews in Egypt abhored Pharaoh's tyranny and the foolishness of idolatrous worships. Yet, not as far as not keeping within their hearts some attachment to the onions, garlics and meats of that country. They left, finally, and entered the desert where they were fed with a prodigious food, the manna from heaven. Do you think they were happy with that?... On the contrary, they began reminiscing those foods and longed for them. Thus, they kept losing the savour of the manna that came down from heaven. Finally they wanted to satiate themselves with that meat and, filling themselves to the excess, many of them died from it miserably. Others, who perhaps did not feed themselves with that meat but longed for it, little by little moved into more serious faults of coveting, murmuring, and slandering. Little by little they became idolaters. Would you believe it? Of the people seen moving out of Egypt into the desert in the midst of so many wonders, many were found to prostrate themselves before the god of pagan matter.

Now, brag, saying that to keep a little attachment or ambition is only a slight matter. It is an evil which can cause the sadest consequences. A puncture in the heart can be deadly, a cold that is not cared for can cause pneumonia, a simple cut can turn into a painful and poisoned sore that leads to the agony of death. What do you say now? Don't say any more that a venial sin is a slight matter. It may become a very serious evil. Let us all see to it that we are completely cleansed in our hearts, which after all is the best way to be.

REFLECTIONS

1. Is your heart pure?
2. Do you cleanse your heart or you just clean it?
3. See to it that the dust of harmful thoughts does not lay on it.
4. It would be enough to bring your soul to death.

GOSPEL OF THE FIFTEENTH SUNDAY AFTER PENTECOST

Sound of universal shaking

1. At the sound of divine will heaven and earth were created from nothing. At the sound of the voice of Jesus Christ stormy waters quieted down, the sick were cured, the dead were brought back to life. Listen to what today's Gospel says.

"Soon afterward Jesus went to a town called Naim, and his disciples and a large crowd accompanied him. As he approached the gate of the town a dead man was being carried out, the only son of a widowed mother. A considerable crowd of townsfolk were with her. The Lord was moved with pity upon seeing her and said to her, 'Do not cry.' Then he stepped forward and touched the litter; at this, the bearers halted. He said, 'Young man, I bid you get up.' The dead man sat up and began to speak. Then Jesus gave him back to his mother. Fear seized them all and they began to praise god. 'A great prophet has risen among us,' they said; and, 'God has visited his people.'"[1]

The sound of Jesus Christ's voice raises the dead of Palestine. At the sound of his cry the universe will shake. Really not him, but an angel in the name of the Lord will sound the trumpet. St. John writes: "...an hour is coming in which all those in their tombs shall hear the voice of the Son of God and come forth. Those who have done right shall rise

---

[1] Lk 7:11-16

to live; the evildoers shall rise to be damned."[1] Let us examine thoroughly the terror of this trumpet's voice, for at its sound heaven and earth will be shaken.

2. The voice of a powerful king is always a commanding voice. The ancient Hebrews were accustomed to receive the order of command from their sovereign at the sound of a trumpet. At the sound of a trumpet the great assembly of the nation was gathered. At the sound of the trumpet war was waged against the neighboring adversaries. At the sound of the trumpet people assembled for the feasts and at the sound of the trumpet they broke camp and pitched their tents from place to place.

The sound of the trumpet will soon one day resound in all parts of the earth. The command to sound the trumpet will be given by Jesus Christ, the king of the universe. One of his angels, his ministers, will sound it. Everyone will hear the voice of that trumpet. The sound will be heard by those who today are so reluctant to listening to the voice of the preacher or of the confessor. It will be heard by those who today close both ears in order not to hear the advise of a friend. Even those who, in order not to hear the importuning voice of a prophet, try to kill them all, will hear the voice of the Son of God. They will hear it even after being dead for a thousand years. They will hear it and, carrying out its command, they will all gather to give account of their conduct.

3. Then at last, men will be seen as they have been in their lives. Now we do not know it. Good people live along with the evil ones. Often times the evil ones prosper and stroll about like gods here on earth. Yet the time of justice has

---

[1] Jn 5:28-29

come. The elect, then, will come forth to the resurrection of life. They will be light, radiant, greatly dear to God, glorious to behold by all.

The evildoers, also, will rise, and they will come forth for the resurrection of condemnation. I cannot tell you how fetid, heavy, and horrible they will be, because they will rise to be mixed together with the damned in hell! What a change! Faithful of the Lord, do not ever envy the impious. Seeing them, have pity for them and pray for them. If there is only one evildoer here among you, may he open up his eyes and observe the condemnation that hangs over him. Let us be servants of the Lord. It is fitting that God at last one day will do inexorable justice.

4. All will gather at the sound of that trumpet. The elect, in order of rank, will ascend on high to meet Jesus Christ their savior. The reprobates in order of wickedness will stay on earth waiting for him to come.

Once Federick I (Barbarossa), after taking over the city of Pavia, threatened to exterminate the city of Milan. The citizens of this city went to meet him to implore for mercy! It was too late. Frederick went and destroyed the city, had its ruins all covered with salt, and surrounded by farming carts.

At the sight of Jesus' coming the reprobates will come forth with great lamentations, yet there is no time for mercy at that hour. It is written that mercy is kept for man as long as he lives here below. After he dies, at the time of judgment, justice will be severe and inexorable.

The reprobates will see themselves separated from the elect, and will realize that there is no way of being spared. They are separated for ever. The just will applaud with their voices, with their hands, and will say: "You are just, O Lord, and upright are the ways of your justice." It is a sign of glory for a king to be able to set aside the rebels in order to punish them. The reprobates will hear all this while waiting for the voice of condemnation awaiting them.

5. At the moment of universal judgment everyone pays attention to nothing but the good or evil each has done. No matter how an individual may be, poor and in rags and tatters, ignorant and wretched, yet if he has walked with simplicity in the presence of God, he will indeed be saved. Others who, though rich and powerful, lofty and learned in human sciences, yet have neglected doing good and have done evil, these will be condemned without exception.

Go, now, and trust the judgment of men! Have confidence in the great ones of the earth! Envy the powerful and the glorious! Fools! Fools! If they do not do what is truly good according to faith and religion, they work in vain. On the Lord's final judgment day human greatness means nothing. What good will it be to bring to attention the bravery of Hanibal, the knowledge of Archimedes, the philosophy of Aristotle? At the judgment the poverty of St. Francis of Assisi will be appreciated, as well as the humility of St. Pasqual Baylon, the true knowledge of St. Thomas Aquinas, and the philosophy yes, but the Christian one, of the holy Fathers. This is valued. Other than that, there is nothing but deception and perdition. Did you understand how at the sound of the voice of the Son of God, heaven and earth will shake? Let us fear that voice, let all of us fear it.

RESOLUTIONS

1. The voice of universal shaking.
2. The sound of the trumpet at the final resurrection.
3. At the sound of that voice the elect will gather as well as the reprobates themselves.
4. They will gather in ranks.
5. At God's judgment nothing is taken into account other than the good or evil one has committed.

GOSPEL OF THE SIXTEENTH SUNDAY
AFTER PENTECOST

A candidate for the army

1. You have before your eyes Jesus Christ, a valiant captain, knowledgeable and resourceful, who leads his people to a sure victory. He hands to you powerful weapons, prayer, the holy Sacraments, the good deeds. He leads you in person. The enemies you have to battle are within yourselves, that is your concupiscences are Christ's enemies and Satan's ministers here in this world. The adversaries are the spirits of hell.

Do you want to join the banned of Jesus? Pay attention to the motto written on it. On one side you read *Abstine (Abstain)*. On the other side, *Sustine (Bear with)*. Contrast that motto with what the holy Gospel of this Sunday says.

"When you are invited by someone to a wedding party, do not sit in the place of honor in case some greater dignitary has been invited. Then the host might come and say to you, 'Make room for this man,' and you would have to proceed shamefacedly to the lowest place. What you should do when you have been invited is go and sit in the lowest place, so that when your host approaches you he will say, 'My friend, come up higher.' This will win you the esteem of your fellow guests. For everyone who exalts himself shall be humbled and he who humbles himself shall be exalted."[1]

Here you find in this passage of the gospel a lesson on how to conduct yourself wisely following the banner of the

---

[1] Lk 14:8-11

divine Savior. Do you want to join with a willing heart? Listen to what the Lord suggests in the book of *Sirach*: "My son, when you come to serve the Lord, prepare yourself for trials."[1] Let us ponder upon this discourse immediately, because we do not want to delay joining the army of Jesus.

2. All the Christians who gather under the banner of Jesus must fight. The newcomers as well as the soldiers on the battlefield and even the veterans must fight. As long as we wear the arms we have to fight. Wasn't Jesus most perfect and holy on his own? Yet he wanted to undergo so many trials and temptations to teach all of us that to undergo a temptation in any state in life is not a shame but an honor, because it is an invitation to fight continuously so as to triumph.

While all soldiers are expected to fight, the new recruits are the ones who have to be willing to bear with the greatest sufferings, since they have just left their families. The beginners in the service of the Lord must be prepared in a special way for the trials for two specific reasons. They are young, thereby ill prepared for battles. A second reason is that the devils, whom they have escaped by joining Jesus' banner, wage a harsh and more persistent war against them. Be patient, then, you who long for being the soldiers of Jesus Christ. Find comfort in patience through the many trials.

3. The artifices that Satan will use in battling you will be the same ones Lucifer employed against Jesus Christ. Satan realized that Jesus had been baptized by John the Baptist and afterward had secluded himself in penance in the desert. What did he do next?... He appeared to him to

---

[1] Sir 2:1

sympathize with him for being hungry and weak, suggesting to him to do something that, after all, was not bad. He handed him a few stones and suggested: "Command that these stones turn into bread." It was a temptation of cowardice. The first temptations Satan will hand to you will be asking you to take care of your body, to shun fasting, not to deny any kind of satisfaction to the flesh, otherwise it will get sick or die.

The devil took one more step. He appeared as the angel of light and said: "You can ascend the highest pinnacle of the temple and throw yourself down, for it is written that the angels will defend you." This was a temptation of presumption. Can he tempt the Lord?... At the same time he will also tell you that you have to prove yourself, you have to show your talents; he will tell you that you have to aspire to a role of command to do good, that you have to show that you are wise to lead others to virtue. Deceptions, deceptions! Be content with the admonition that comes from the gospel, and take the last place for yourself, for that is what you deserve. God, if he wants, will call you to a higher place.

Finally Satan dropped the appearance of a man and of an angel and said: "If you prostrate yourself in homage before me, I will make you king of the universe and master of the world."[1] To be a king is the greatest blessing here on earth. A king can flaunt, can give vent to his feelings, can boast as he wants. The devil will also tell you this: "Prostrate yourself before me and I will give you as many pleasures and as much glory as you like." Do you believe him, the liar? Believe him, if so it pleases you. These are the tricks that Satan always uses to damn souls. Do you think that it is better for you to be aware of it?...

---

[1] Mt 4:1-10

4. Take a better look at the devil's art. As soon as you dedicate yourself to a devout way of living, immediately the tempter will prompt you: "Will you able to go to confession so often, to receive communion so often, to guard yourself from the conversation of your worldly companions? And will you be willing to bear with the mockeries and the desertions of people?..." If this temptation does not get through to you, then Lucifer adds: "Well, you have dedicated yourself to the divine service. Everyone applauds you, but then be a faithful servant, spare no fasting, no scourges, no untiring prayer. If you get sick of it, your body will die but your spirit will be saved." The liar speaks in this way to see to it that you get so sick that at the end, losing your patience, you give up the whole thing.

If even this does not help realize his goal, then the tempter drops his mask and furiously comes to you and says: "Crazy ones, what did you do? Don't you miss the great fun that you enjoyed in the world? Go back, crazy ones, go back, for to save your soul it is enough to give to God the last day of your life." Here he appears in his whole impudence and clearly attempts to ruin you. What do you say? Brace yourselves against the malign art of Satan. Realize that he tries little by little to seduce you. Don't give in to him a bit, for it could be for you the beginning of your defeat.

5. Answer back to the assaults of the devil as Jesus did. The best place for you to win in this case is solitude, where more easily you can invoke the Lord. If there the devil tempts you to be a coward by saying: "How can you always conduct a devout life?...", answer back with a sincere, firm and authoritative voice: "Not on bread alone is man to live, but on every word that comes from the mouth of God." The Lord is with you, who can hurt you? Or what can you lack that is

necessary? If you lack one sort of food, you find another kind. In the desert there was no ordinary food, and so God sent the manna.

Another time the devil tempts you with presumption by saying: "Get involved with a lot of devotions so that you may become a saint quickly." Answer back that God is not obliged to make miracles by carrying you bodily while you can progress little by little on your own feet. You must not tempt the Lord.

Finally, if Lucifer says to you: "Go back to the pleasures of the earth, for I give them to you all together and for a while," answer: "What can you give to me, wretched thief, miserable beast, chained dog? Liar, liar! Get away from me!" Tell him over and over again to leave you, get lost, and not to dare to appear before you again. In this way you have won all your battles. The angels of the Lord will come to you to rejoice with you and you will be saved at last.

REFLECTIONS

1. An aspirant soldier.
2. All the soldiers of Jesus Christ must be tried, but especially the new recruits.
3. The warfare arts of Satan are cowardice, presumption, and open rebellion.
4. He tempts everyone with these approaches.
5. You fight him back with opposite approaches, as Jesus Christ did, and you will be saved and victorious.

GOSPEL OF THE SEVENTEENTH SUNDAY AFTER PENTECOST

A staged glory

1. You sit in front of a stage. You see personages coming and going and people boasting about being members of the king's court, the assistant at the throne of the emperor. They show themselves ostentatious in their appearance, proud of their titles. Later on you meet them on the street and you do not recognize them. You ask: "Who are they?" The answer comes: "They are comedians who have done their part." Here you see them, scanty beggars. What do you say? Behold the worldly vanities, they are staged glories.

You appear on the stage of this world. You see politicians who attempt to envelope the world in a net of treason. You see individuals who care for nothing but enrichment for themselves. You see merrymakers longing for pleasures who surround themselves with a lot of people looking for applause. Even these get crazy for the glories of the stage, similar to the Sadducees of today's Gospel who, in order to trap Jesus Christ in his speech and boast about tripping him, asked him: "Which commandment of the Law is the greatest?" Like those Pharisees who, questioned by Jesus concerning whose son they thought he was, answered, "David's." The Savior then retorted: "Then how is it that David under the Spirit's influence calls him 'lord', as he does: 'The Lord said to my lord, Sit at my right hand, until I humble your enemies beneath your feet'? If David calls him 'lord', how can he be his son?' No one could give him an answer;

therefore no one dared, from that day on, to ask him any question."[1]

Thus the audacity and miserable pride of the proud of this century is confounded. What is their greatness? It is a staged glory. "I saw," says the Psalmist, "a wicked man, fierce, and stalwart as a flourishing, age-old tree. Yet as I passed by, lo! he was no more; I sought him, but he could not be found."[2] Then you tell me that the glory of this century is worth a bit. It is a staged glory. Let us look at it and be confounded by it.

2. Let us travel with our minds to the capital cities of the Asian Kingdom, to the ancient Babylon, Tyre, Sidon, Ecbatana. In those times those metropolices were centers of all pleasures. On the towers of the cities flew the flags of all the parts of the known world. The palaces of the great ones were golden. Those personages, like gods here on earth, ruled over everyone and thousands of slaves bowed their faces to the ground, running ahead to level the mountains, filling the valleys, laying aqueducts and channels, planting gardens on terraces up as high as the clouds. All the while the sovereigns strolled in their midst looking down on the crowds kneeling at their passage, seeing to it that they would call them powerful gods as the Lord of heaven.

Miserable, miserable! Where is your power? Are you not a bunch of frail flesh? Where is your knowledge? You are the most stupid ones, for you make yourselves superior to God! Where is at least the prudence of your governing and the love for commanding? You keep nations in slavery and govern them with an iron rod! Miserable, miserable! As you

---

[1] Mt 22:34-36
[2] Ps 37 (36):35-36

are miserable, so are also the great ones of our times. They pretend to be illustrious, yet they are not at all.

Behold, how they fell! There is only a memory left of them. There is not even a trace left of their lofty cities. It is impossible to figure out the precise location of the palaces, and even of the capital city of the king of Babylon! What do you think of this? Are you still going to envy the impious man who is being over-exalted? He is over-exalted, indeed, beyond his merit, therefore unjustly.

3. Is this over-exaltation good for anything, anyway? It is a staged exaltation. It fades away quickly. Caesar Augustus, more than all the other Roman emperors, reigned with a peaceful ruling for the period of fifty-seven years. Realizing he was at the end of his life, he donned his best clothes, combed his hair and then said: "Have I performed well on the scene of this world?... Clap your hands, then! The show is over." Speaking thus, he passed away. Where is glory now?... It was a glory on a stage, which fades away by the same token it is performed.

Here you are admiring a body of water falling down from a mountain, splashing all around and foaming in an enjoyable whiteness arrayed with the magnificent colors of the rainbow. You look at it from top to bottom wishing you could see where the water flowing at that very moment comes from. Yet the water does not stay still. By the time you say: "Here it is!", the awesome churning water has already gone by, falling into the abyss. Think of glory as the column of smoke rising from the chimney. Glory is like the mist rising from the ground after the rain. While it spreads around, it fades away. *Sic transit gloria mundi.* Thus goes the glory of the world! It fades away like smoke and mist. Are we still going to value the glory of the world, that is only a staged glory? Furthermore, are we going to get crazy about this staged glory so as to sacrifice any good for our soul?

4. Looking at vanities like this, what are you going to do? Flee from them, flee from them. Lingering in your mind on that rich merchant who from nothing has climbed into a golden carriage, it might stir envy within. Don't you realize that that same individual has made so many poor people suffer because of his deceptions, that has betrayed so many trusting people with his doubledealings? Get away from them, get away from them. Admiring those rich palaces you might be tempted to say: "How just the Lord is!..." Don't you realize that those edifices and liveries have cost unjust sweat to the poor, and that probably they have been built with the funds sacrilegiously taken from the goods of the Church?... Do you still envy them?...

Don't look at them any further. It is a temptation for you to linger on them. You don't reason with temptation. You don't converse with the devil. The glory of the world is a pitiful scene that ends up with killing the body and delivering the soul into the jaws of hell. Flee, then. Run away from the glories of the world. They are scenes on a stage and displays of sin and damnation. Approach, now, those golden sepulchers. Ask the bodies rotting inside of them: "Did you get any profit from living in the midst of so many softnesses?... Then question the souls already tormented in hell: "Did the glory of the world do any good to you?... Did the pride of life profit you in any way?" They will shout back to you in desperation: "Miserable we were who strayed away from the path of truth. Most miserable are we, for now we are damned forever!"

5. Now try to find them on earth. It's impossible to find them. They have left those palaces, they have disappeared from the theaters, cannot be found in the galleries, nor in the arenas, nor at the games in places of entertainment, glamorous though they might be. They disappeared. Looking at the vanities they have left behind, how confused and sorrowful we should be!

It is useful to look at the vanities that are gone. They have faded away like vapors. They have melted like snow in the sun. In summary, vanities have gone and gone for good. I say it again, where are the palaces of the Romans, the Medes, the Macedonians, the Assyrians? Where are the monarchs who ruled there? The sites of the capital cities cannot be found, never mind the location of their palaces and their coat-of-arms. They have disappeared and no one knows where their dwellings were. Like them, where are now the glories of so many families that made themselves feared even in our own towns? They are gone. What happened to the signs of their nobilities, and the gold of their riches? These are gone, too, or better, they are gone into the hands of dilapidating neighbors or grasping far-away individuals.

Still, we go crazy seeking after human grandeurs? Let us not give a look at them, or let us look at them only to despise them in the recesses of our hearts.

REFLECTIONS

1. A staged glory.
2. The impious do not deserve the honor they claim for themselves.
3. What they enjoy is only a spectacle of foolish vanity.
4. Let us muddle through without even looking at it.
5. Or, if we want to step back, let us do so only to pity those who went astray.

GOSPEL OF THE EIGHTEENTH SUNDAY AFTER PENTECOST

A test to know men

1. A test is very useful in order to ascertain the value of things. At the testing bench analysers determine the quality of gold, the worth of gems, the pure or adulterated quality of foods and drinks. An accurate method of testing is greatly reliable. Now you are going to be very grateful to me for pointing out to you an accurate test to know people. However, you should not be grateful to me for that, but to the Lord, for he is the one who offers this test to you.

Writing to the Ephesians on God's behalf, St. Paul said: "Never let evil talk pass your lips; say only the good things men need to hear, things that will really help them."[1] What the Apostle says goes along with what we gather from the holy Gospel. Listen to the full text from the gospel.

"Then Jesus reentered the boat, made the crossing, and came back to his own town. There the people at once brought to him a paralyzed man lying on a mat. When Jesus saw their faith he said to the paralytic, 'Have courage, son, your sins are forgiven.' At that some of the scribes said to themselves, 'The man blasphemes.' Jesus was aware of what they were thinking and said: 'Why do you harbor evil thoughts? Which is less trouble to say, 'Your sins are forgiven' or 'Stand up and walk'? To help you realize that the Son of Man has authority on earth to forgive sins - he then said to the paralyzed man - 'Stand up! Roll your mat, and go home.'

---

[1] Eph 4:29

The man stood up and went toward his home. At the sight, a feeling of awe came over the crowd, and they praised God for giving such authority to men."[1]

Let us focus our attention on the malignancy of those who, seeing Jesus forgiving sins, kept on murmuring within and openly with everyone. What does this prove? It shows the rotten vice that is in the heart. Do you want to know who you really are and who are the ones who surround you?... Look at the discourses that they usually keep. A test to know individuals is what they usually talk about.

2. A good individual conducts himself so well as is recounted about the youth Lucian, who eventually became a martyr. His contemporaries say that his face was always smiling, his words kind, his spirit even and dear, and that in his demeanor he showed such wisdom and perfection that Christians were edified and moved to do good and the pagans themselves were inspired to conversion.

How is your demeanor? Do you speak gently? Do you always bear the sweetness of kindness on your lips? Do you keep a conversation that is pure and modest? Do you also see to it that you are charitable toward your neighbor? St. Augustine, a bishop, had written on the wall of his hall that whoever wanted to attack the reputation of his neighbor should keep in mind that was not the place to do so. Thus he reprimanded rigorously every word he happened to hear in that place that was less than charitable. Would you be easy to criticize, more willing to blame, or very easy to even slander?

Observe how your conversation goes in speaking about God, the holy religion of Jesus Christ, the pope, the priests,

---

[1] Mt 9:1-8

the Sacraments. St. Teresa said that she was very willing to die to support the dignity of any rite of the holy Church.

Brothers and sisters, brothers and sisters! When one's breath stinks, it means that his stomach is infected. It does not help justifying oneself by claiming that the conversation keeps on going without meaning it. Don't you have the door, your lips, and the locks, your teeth, to prevent you from keeping evil conversations? Avail yourselves of them.

3. Let us all be good Christians, let us be perfect Christians! We have so much evil to make reparation for, so many sinners to save, so much glory to procure for Jesus Christ. Let us keep good conversations to edify our neighbor and to save souls. Let us keep those conversations not with affectation, but with sincerity of heart. Not out of ambition, but out of charity. Our neighbor should not even be aware of the charity we are doing to him with our pious discourse.

We read in Sacred Scripture that Booz, seeing from a distance the poor Ruth gleaning after the harvesters, told them: "Let many ears of wheat fall abundantly and even leave behind handfuls of them, so that the poor woman's heart be consoled." Let us imitate this behavior. A conversation kept with authority loses its meaning. A conversation done with affectation or artificiality is not enjoyed. Your conversation must be carried on with the right intention, and come from the bottom of your heart. Oh, if many people would keep holy conversations, how much more easily the world of the evil and indifferent people would be converted!

4. Thus a good conversation benefits those who begin doing good to others as a restoring food benefits the convalescents recovering from a serious illness. Good conversations benefit the good Christians as the loaves of

bread restored Elijah the prophet so he could reach Mt. Horeb after a journey of forty days.

Good coversations benefit the perfect Christians as the sound of the organ and the harmonious chanting of pious youths who in the holy temple give unceasing praise to the majesty of the Lord. All along those conversations refresh with joy as one would feel being in the antichamber of paradise. They clear up the mind, comfort the heart, add zest to the body.

Very fortunate is the Christian who is able to keep up with good and edifying conversation. He lives here on earth as a blessing, is greeted with joy by the angels in paradise. He lives here on earth as an angel and savior to comfort and rescue others. How do you feel about it? Isn't it a great surprise how a simple Christian individual can do so much good among men? We will be fortunate if we will see to it that our lips do not utter evil conversations, but always good ones.

REFLECTIONS

1. A test to know men.
2. What kind of conversations do we carry on in regard to ourselves, our neighbor or God?
3. Let us then converse with edification.
4. We will benefit from it ourselves, as so will everyone else.

GOSPEL OF THE NINETEENTH SUNDAY AFTER PENTECOST

A bit of light

1. My brothers and sisters, let us kindle around us at least a bit of light. The envious want to deprive us of it completely. The light of the day is so abundant and for everyone; why do now the liberals of today hang around arrogantly and tyrantly threatening us if we look up high? They want us to look down low. They become angry if they see that someone does not put his muzzle into earthly pleasures, but turns his Christian face up on high. It has been that way. The sensual merrymakers have always waged war to spiritual Christians. Listen to what the holy Gospel says in this regard.

Jesus began to address them, once more using parables. "The reign of God may be likened to a king who gave a wedding banquet for his son. He dispatched his servants to summon the invited guests to the wedding, but they refused to come. A second time he sent other servants, saying: 'Tell those who were invited, See, I have my dinner prepared! My bullocks and corn-fed cattle are killed; everything is ready. Come to the feast.' Some ignored the invitation and went their way, one to his farm, another to his business. The rest laid hold of his servants, insulted them, and killed them. At this the king grew furious and sent his army to destroy those murderers and burn their city. Then he said to his servants: 'The banquet is ready, but those who were invited were unfit to come. That is why you must go out into the byroads and invite to the wedding anyone you come upon.' The servants then went out into the byroads and rounded up everyone they met, bad as well as good. This filled the wedding hall with banqueters.

When the king came in to meet the guests, however, he caught sight of a man not properly dressed for a wedding feast. 'My friend,' he said, 'how is it you came in here not properly dressed?' The man had nothing to say. The king then said to the attendants, 'Bind him hand and foot and throw him out into the night to wail and grind his teeth.' The invited are many, the elect are few."[1]

This Gospel's lesson enlightens us in our way. The proud, the sensual and the greedy prefer to roll in the mire better than sit at the table of a holy king. Not us, not us! We want to adhere to what St. Paul suggests along with the sacred Gospel, when, writing to the Philippians, he said: "Those things I used to consider gain I have now reappraised as loss in the light of Christ. I have come to rate all as loss in the light of the surpassing knowledge of my Lord, Jesus Christ. For his sake I have forfeited everything; I have accounted all else rubbish so that Christ may be my wealth."[2]

What a light in the discourse of the apostle! Let us look at it to admire it, because in this splendor there are rays of divine light capable of scattering the darkness of the world.

2. Let us focus on a concrete example. A baby perceives the first rays of the sun coming through the window reaching him laying in the crib, and tries to catch them. Then he sees a toy and is willing to give up everything to get that. Grown a little, he sees a butterfly, or a fire-fly and here he runs quickly after them. He leaves his mother and father to

---

[1] Mt 22:1-14
[2] Phil 3:7ff

run after those most futile things. A grown-up adult, he scours the world purchasing items he considers precious, like pearls, paintings, and objects of classic art. Then he comes home in triumph, yet, what a disappointment! What he thought it were precious pearls are not but mere crystal, and the best of the paintings or objects of art are nothing but useless items worthy of being thrown into the fire. What a sad disappointment! At last he learns what his wise father had taught him a long time back, and then hitting his head, he says: "What a foolish and blind man I have been, running around in the darkness, while I had the light of a perfect guide here at home!"

Think now of how worldly people, who follow the vanity of earthly pleasures and glories, should be regarded with greater indulgence than the foolish child mentioned above! They will realize when God gives them the grace to open up their eyes. Lord, enlighten us all! Foolish is he who leaves the light from heaven in order to grope in the darkness of this earth!

3. Whatever comes from the earth is gloomy. Human knowledge, human glory as well as power and riches, everything is equally thick darkness. Therefore no wonder if so much of the world is the darkness, because almost everyone has his heart plunged into this darkness.

One of the wise people saw to it that he might have some light. It was St. Francis of Assisi. As soon as he discovered the splendor of the light coming from the poverty of Bethlehem, he immediately looked to it, and kept his eyes on it for ever. When he saw the light coming from Jesus preaching on the famous mountain, he quickly retained the brightness of the discourse that said: "Blessed are they who long to see God, blessed are they who weep and suffer persecution for Jesus Christ's sake." Seeing Jesus on the cross exclaiming: "I thirst for more sufferings", St. Francis, too, kept on longing for martyrdom. Not getting it, he at least wanted to experience the martyrdom of the sacred wounds of the divine Savior. What do you say?... Oh, I wish you had seen St. Francis speak, had seen him walk!... His discourses spread a torrent of light, his presence was a sun of real splendor.

May the Lord grant us the grace to perceive the person and doctrine of Jesus Christ, then how heartily we would detest the darkness of this earth! A little bit of light, my brothers and sisters! Let us beg to obtain from above at least a bit of light for our eyes.

4. We will realize, like the Apostle St. Paul, that the goods here below are not to be valued but only to be shunned like the stench of excrements. In the Sacred Scriptures we read that the pleasures of the sensual are likened to the excrements of vile pack-horses, because of the stench that they spread tainting themselves and others. The pleasures of the stingy individual are likened to the excrements of the cows because of the laziness by which those animals adhere to the soil. The glories of the greedy are likened to excrements filled with worms because they stink more than any other pestiferous stench. Did you ever see a drove of dogs rushing to feed themselves on the bowels of a disemboweled animal? They get into them with much more pleasure because the odor coming out of those exposed intestines is very acute.

Vanities of avarice and sensuality or pride are very fetid excrements. Where was anyone found to be so attached to such excrement, as to long for having it close at home?... As a matter of fact, he who cannot get rid of it, must desire to stay away from it as much as possible. Yet there are

Christians who plunge into it with great pleasure, they breathe it, and live on it. Miserable, miserable! They leave Jesus Christ aside to plunge into that stench. Such blindness would be unbelievable if unfortunately it were not true.

5. Is this the way human beings esteem Jesus Christ?... Yet we who are Christians will think differently. A faithful Christian longs for nothing but Jesus Christ. He finds everything in the adorable person of Jesus. Take a look at St. Paul the Apostle. Out of his love for Jesus he renounced the prejudice of worldly honor and merited to intimately penetrate the most secret mysteries of his adorable heart. Listen to what the Apostle was able to say afterwards. He said: "The life I live now is not my own; Christ is living in me."[1]

St. Francis of Assisi presented himself to his bishop deprived of everything, eager only to follow the divine Savior. He profited immensely from it. St. Francis was elevated to such a lofty degree of humility and trust in God that he looked like another Jesus Christ. Look at him: Francis is poor as Jesus was, persecuted as Jesus was, wounded as Jesus was, and like Jesus he had his heart burning with fires of desire and holy love. Christians, Christians, this is a pleasure, this is a gain. Ah, why doesn't the world look at places and people shining with such a splendor of good example? A bit of light, O Lord, to us too! Oh, that a bit of light from heaven may descend to scatter this darkness!

---

[1] Gal 2:20

REFLECTIONS

1. A bit of light.
2. Are earthly goods to be desired?
3. They are so gloomy!
4. As a matter of fact they are vile like excrement.
5. How much better it is for us to cling to Jesus Christ!

GOSPEL OF THE TWENTIETH SUNDAY AFTER PENTECOST

Merchants of time

1. The most famous merchants of all men are those who deal with the most precious goods. Now of whatever we have here on earth, undoubtedly precious is the time that God has granted us and still gives us for the time being. Let us take advantage of it for our sake, thus we will be not only illustrious but fortunate merchants, which means much more. We are led to this by the royal official mentioned in today's Gospel.. Pay attention to grasp not only the general sense but even the literal sense of the text as presented to us by St. John.

"At Capernaum there happened to be a royal official whose son was ill. When he heard that Jesus had come back from Judea to Galilee, he went to him and begged him to come down and restore health to his son, who was near death. Jesus replied, 'Unless you people see signs and wonders, you do not believe.' 'Sir,' the royal official pleaded with him, 'come down before my child dies.' Jesus told him, 'Return home. Your son will live.' The man put his trust in the word Jesus spoke to him, and started for home. He was on his way there when his servants met him with the news that his boy was going to live. When he asked them at what time the boy had shown improvement, they told him, 'The fever left him yesterday afternoon about one.' It was at that very hour, the father realized, that Jesus had told him, 'Your son is going to live.' He and his whole household thereupon became believers."[1]

Most noble father who, upon perceiving dangerous days for his son, hastened to drive the danger away! Gloomy are the days of our life here below. We have to spend them in the midst of many dangers. There are robbers who attempt to rob us of the best of the time God grants us to do penance and sanctify ourselves. Let us see to it that we become good merchants of our time. St. Paul says: "Keep careful watch over your conduct. Do not act like fools, but like thoughtful men. Make the most of the present opportunity, for these are evil days."[2]

2. The Lord has given a holy dwelling to his Christians here below, the dwelling of the Most High, a blessed temple. In this temple everyone can sanctify himself, because the church is Mt. Calvary whence the merits of the passion and death of Jesus still flow. As on Mt. Calvary, likewise in the church there may be found people who come to crucify Jesus with scandals, sacrileges, and most evil designs, as the executioners did to the divine Savior. Some people come to church and attend there coldly, as mere onlookers at a show. Others do come to participate as it is expected, that is, to sanctify themselves.

Imagine now that the time of our life is like a blessed church. God has set us in our life time so that we may sanctify ourselves. However, how do people live?... There are Christians who dwell here below wickedly, to sin themselves and make others sin. There are other Christians who dwell with indifference, devoting themselves to every sort of useless

---

[1] Jn 4:46-53
[2] Eph 5:15-16

and most vain undertakings. Finally, there are Christians who, by God's mercy, make use of every second of their time for the glory of God and the perfection of their souls.

To which of these three categories do we belong? Let us keep in mind that living in time is like dwelling in the church of the Lord. In a holy temple a Christian can achieve one of two things, to be sanctified by it or to become worse through iniquities of greater sins.

3. What have we done so far? If conscience reproaches us for misusing time, or for not taking advantage of it as we ought, let us make up for it. What do wayfarers do when they find out that they are lost?... They quickly trace their way back to the path they had abandoned. What do farmers do when they realize they have overslept in the shade of the oak trees?... They put themselves into their work with greater effort.

If they do so for the sake of temporal and passing things, what should we do to our advantage in the real world of spiritual and eternal matters? If we have spent time in sin, let us deplore it with tears as much as possible. If we have wasted time vainly in worldly stupidities, let us now focus on more fervent prayer, performing more vigilant deeds of good. This means to redeem the lost time. He who does not take the trouble to do this is a fool who does not acknowledge his own mistakes.

4. We have said that the time we spend here below is like the hours we spend in a holy temple. Let us reflect on this closely. Whatever surrounds us is holy: the church, the altars, the sacred images. Jesus Christ in the Blessed Sacrament looks at us to measure every good thought in our mind, every good affection in our heart. Besides, see what example of

good virtues and encouragement to do good is given by those good Christians who confess their sins, weep over them, pray and give alms!... Yet, let us guard ourselves against those who stay in church idly, or stay there only to sin. These take the place of Satan and of his ministers. Are the worst Christians any different from those assassins lying in wait for slaughtering?...

Let us be aware, let us be aware. Assassins and tempters are all those impediments that interfere and keep us from spending time holily. Sinful conversations or useless entertainments, waste of time at entertainments, idleness and apathy, this is what should terrify us. Let us guard ourselves against this as against an evildoer who sets a snare for us, as a robber planning on taking our life.

5. Above all, let us guard ourselves against individuals who may be friends of ours willing to make us waste time with chatters, or enemies who want us to waste time in quarrels. Don't get accustomed to gossips. You wouldn't be Christians with solid perfection. Also, do not linger around, wasting your time and peace of mind when someone comes to say nasty things to you or take something that belongs to you. "*Perde aliquid et redime tempus*", says St. Augustine. It is better to lose something that is temporal in order to secure for ourselves much more of what is spiritual and eternal.

We are in a church, the house of the Lord. To be there with attention and savor spiritual sweetnesses it is worthwhile to sacrifice some kind of temporal gain. Here on earth we are in time to sanctify ourselves. The blessed above in paradise, had they the possibility to desire something more, they would long to be able to come back on earth in order to have time to love God more. By the same token, those unfortunate souls down below, they wish they could come out of that abyss of torment to return on earth to redeem their time! Do you think that they would ever miss any means to employ the best way possible every bit of precious time?

6. Yet the time God grants to us is the present we live in, here and now. Let us see to it that we spend it holily right away, because it soon will be no more. After this life there is only one thing, the blessed eternity or the eternity of damnation.

Therefore, let us see to it that we avoid all those dismal encounters that in some way might contribute to damage us by wasting time. He who proceeds causciously is considered wise because he knows how to conduct himself. He who is not aware of dangers is a fool who does not know anything, he is a foolish child. What do you think, then? Let us all handle with prudence this matter that is above everything else. Let us care for the time that God has granted us. Time is the most precious treasure of all. Let us care for being very shrewd merchants. Let us make use of the time granted to us for the purpose of gaining paradise and God.

REFLECTIONS

1. Merchants of time.
2. In the time here on earth we are as in a temple, that is the house of God, to sanctify ourselves.
3. Let us make amends for the evil or useless use of time we have exerted so far.
4. Let us guard ourselves against the assassins of the time granted to us.

5. Let us lose something of temporal goods, yet let us not waste any of the time which is so precious for our salvation.

6. Let us proceed cautiously so that we may avoid all dangerous encounters.

GOSPEL OF THE TWENTY-FIRST
SUNDAY AFTER PENTECOST

Two types of soil

1. In creating man God inspires an immortal breath into the heart of this creature, and thus he gives him the life and power to do good. God gives man the freedom of choice between good and evil. There is a difference, however, which is deplorable, that is while an individual responds to God as a fertile soil, the heart of another responds as the arid soil of a thorn-bush. Miserable is that soil that does not produce any fruits after it has been showered upon by the dew of the divine grace! The holy Gospel gives us an example of these two types of soil. St. Matthew recounts as follows:

Jesus said to his disciples: "That is why the reign of God may be said to be like a king who decided to settle accounts with his officials. When he began his auditing, one was brought in who owed him a huge amount. As he had no way of paying it, his master ordered him to be sold, along with his wife, his children, and all his property, in payment of the debt. At that the official prostrated himself in homage and said, 'My lord, be patient with me and I will pay you back in full.' Moved with pity, the master let the official go and wrote off the debt. But when this same official went out he met a fellow servant who owed him a mere fraction of what he himself owed. He seized him and throttled him. 'Pay back what you owe,' he demanded. His fellow servant dropped to his knees and began to plead with him, 'Just give me time and I will pay you back in full.' But he would hear none of it. Instead, he had him put in jail until he paid back what he owed. When his fellow servants saw what had happened they

234

were badly shaken, and went to their master to report the whole incident. His master sent for him and said, 'You worthless wretch! I canceled your entire debt when you pleaded with me. Should you not have dealt mercifully with your fellow servant, as I dealt with you?' Then in anger the master handed him over to the torturers until he paid back all that he owed. My heavenly Father will treat you in exactly the same way unless each of you forgives his brother from his heart."[1]

The affections of our heart are like a fertile soil in a garden or like the sterile soil in an uncultivated plot of land. What is going to happen to these two very different types of soil? Certainly they will end at two opposite destinations. Writing to the Hebrews, St. Paul says: "Ground which drinks in the rain falling on it again and again, and brings forth vegetation useful to those for whom it is cultivated, receives the blessing of God. But if it bears thorns and thistles, it is worthless; it is soon cursed, and finally is burned."[2] Here we see how different is the destiny that falls on each of these two grounds. Let us take a look at it closely and be horrified by it.

2. I make use of one example to show you the difference of two soils equally cultivated. There are hearts that respond to grace, and these are blessed. There are others that do not respond at all, and these are cursed.

Two young men, Gregory and Julian, lived simultaneously and attended the same school. The first one, the child of honest parents, the second a close descendant of Constantine the Great. The same dew fell on both of them, the good grace of a Christian wise education. Gregory responded and was always a good Christian young man, then a pious

---

[1] Mt 18:23-35
[2] Heb 6:7-8

priest, and finally an intrepid bishop. All along he was an excellent preacher, Doctor and Father of the holy Church, who gained souls for the kingdom of Christ by his example and writings. What a fertile soil was Gregory's heart!

Not so Julian's heart. This one responded badly and became a most wicked persecutor of Christian religion. He began to say: "Christians must believe blindly", and denied them the benefit of education, removed them from all branches of government and administration. Then he added: "Christians must love being poor", and confiscated all their goods. Finally, he kept saying: "They must be persecuted", and kept wounding them to death. He wanted to give the lie to Jesus Christ himself. So he said: "Jesus said that the temple of Jerusalem couldn't be rebuilt any more, yet I will raise it more magnificent than ever and thus Jesus Christ will be proven a lier." He tried, yet mysterious flames rose to burn to ashes the workers. In the meantime emperor Julian was forced to wage war on the Persians. Realizing that he was losing, he drove a knife into his chest. The blood gushed out vehemently. Julian filled the hollow of his hand with it and throwing it up high he blasphemed: "You won, O Galilean!" Then he immediately died.

My brothers and sisters, is the soil of our heart grateful or ungrateful? If it does not respond to the benefits of God it will certainly become a cursed soil.

3. Good as a soil may be, it does not produce fruits unless God sends his rain upon it from heaven. Very fertile was the land of Palestine, but in the times of Elijah no rain fell upon it for three years. Not a blade of grass could grow in it. Do you when God gave rain abundantly? It was when Elijah worked the miracle narrated in the Sacred Books, because of which King Ahab ackowledged the Lord of

heaven. A cloud rose then as small as a man's hand above Mt. Carmel. It grew and grew so as to cover all the skies above and a heavy rain fell to restore the parched land.

This is what the grace of the Lord does to the recesses of a soul. Without it, our soul is like a soil without water. What are we expected to do? It is left to us to cry out to God with love and affection: "Without you, O Lord, my heart is like soil without water!"[1]

4. On his part, however, how many graces God has already given to us! He has sent streams of holy inspirations upon us. What use have we made of them? St. Ignatius received a stream of grace during the siege of Pamplona when his foot was wounded. St. Ignatius used it to become a saint. Even Luther received a stream of grace when he was spared from a lightning that burned his travel companion. Luther, however, did not restrain himself from becoming an apostate and minister of Satan for the ruin of so many souls.

How we ourselves should be ashamed! If we had responded to divine graces we would have grown greatly in perfection. Yet we are so miserable because we have been so ungrateful.

5. What have we produced so far? If we have produced good fruits, let us be happy with it, for paradise will be our reward for it. If we have produced prickles, an image of our mortal though minor sins, or brambles, an image of more serious sins, then let us tremble. What we deserve is eternal damnation. Both the act of recompense and condemnation come from above. The choice depends on the good deeds or evil deeds we have committed.

---

[1] Ps 143(142):6

Out of the twelve apostles of the Lord, one, the traitor, made himself worthy of condemnation. Among the first twelve disciples of St. Francis one turned out to be a traitor of religion and perished miserably. All the others were saved. Lord, Lord, see to it that all of us at least do good consistently so as to be saved.

6. Ah, a sterile soil must be prepared for a terrible punishment! God has rejected it since the beginning because he found it unfruitful. He then cursed it, for there is no reason for a soil to be tolerated if it does not produce good fruits. A ground with thisles and thorns is burned.

In this sense, after they condemned to death the divine Savior, the Hebrews were rejected, and then were cursed because of the great iniquity they had committed. Finally they were handed to the flames during the destruction of Jerusalem. Read the historian Joseph Flavius' account and fail to tremble, if you can.

7. Ah, a soul that like parched land rejects the heavenly graces, is a sign that it has been rejected. It will soon be cursed and then condemned to burn. Finally observe the land washed by the waters of the sacred river, Jordan. These watered lands multiply their fruits. Yet this is not the case of the lands beyond the Jordan, that deserved the torrents of flames that fell upon them. They disappeared and seemed to join the abyss of hell. Don't you think, then, that it is better to be like a soil that responds to divine graces? Let us all be upright and grateful! May heaven assist us to remain that way till the end.

REFLECTIONS

1. Two soils.
2. Difference of how the soil of two Christian hearts respond to the rain of heavenly favors.
3. Rain always comes from above.
4. It falls abundantly.
5. It makes the soil produce, then, fruits of good deeds or thisles of sins or thorns of iniquities.
6. The sterile soil receives a triple punishment.
7. Streams of graces rain upon good hearts, while ungrateful hearts receive streams of flames.

GOSPEL OF THE TWENTY-SECOND SUNDAY AFTER PENTECOST

Let the mask come down!

1. Tell the politicians of our times: "Take off your mask!" Tell our brothers in our country who protest to be fathers and instead are step-fathers, to be brothers and instead are tyrants. Tell them: "Take off your mask otherwise the Lord will take it from you!", for a crime of hypocrisy or treason ruining so many souls cannot continue for too long without being punished.

Beware of them, my brothers and sisters, yet be not scandalized by these hypocrites. There have always been liars in the midst of human beings. They have been numerous and evil even when the Savior himself appeared to bring down the kingdom of sin. St. Matthew the Evangelist today reminds us of the following:

"Then the Pharisees went off and began to plot how they might trap Jesus in speech. They sent their disciples to him, accompanied by Herodian sympathizers, who said: 'Teacher, we know you are a truthful man and teach God's way sincerely. You court no one's favor and do not act out of human respect. Give us your opinion, then, in this case. Is it lawful to pay tax to the emperor or not?' Jesus recognized their bad faith and said to them, 'Why are you trying to trip me up, you hypocrites? Show me the coin used for the tax.' When they handed him a small Roman coin he asked them, 'Whose head is this, and whose inscription?' 'Caesar's,' they replied. At that he said to them, 'Then give to Caesar what is Caesar's, but give to God what is God's.'"[1]

How did the divine Savior really take off the mask from those hypocrites. He couldn't stand them, the divine Savior, the impostors! He called them whited sepulchers, brood of vipers, the miserable ones for whom the wrath of the Lord was set ready. Are the evil ones going to prosper forever?... St. Paul writes to the Corinthians: "The work of each will be made clear. The Day will disclose it. That day will make its appearance with fire, and fire will test the quality of each man's work."[2]

My brothers and sisters, we, too, have the need to be called in the presence of ourselves and of God. Let us see to it that we find out to what extent our fidelity in the service of the Lord goes. The evil ones will be certainly punished, and while we feel bad for them, let us not be taken over by fear.

2. Iniquitous individuals have their day in which they can give vent to their whims of revenge or cruelty. Nero and Caligolas, Diocletian down to Decius, have carried out in their days of furor great revenge over innocent Christian people. God let them alone for a while. Yet, the Lord who is just and holy, picks his own time to show his justice.

The days of the Lord are three in a special way. The first day is the day of the universal judgment, called the great day. How will all hypocrites tremble on that day, all the iniquitous and evil ones! The second day will be on the day of the individual judgment that takes place right after death. What a terrible thing on that day to appear for the first time before the Most High! The third day is during life, when he

---

[1] Mt 22:15-21
[2] 1 Cor 3:13

appears at the time of tribulation. As fire tries gold, so tribulation is a test for judgment.

Do you want to know how we will be found at the time of the particular or the universal judgment? We will be at the same degree of virtue or weakness we show in the days of tribulation. My brothers and sisters, when the time of tribulation comes, oh how fearful we should be, because if we do not stand the trial, we are done with, then.

3. Today there are adulterers and dissolute individuals who know how to pretend, who in the sight of the public look like pure angels. There are greedy oppressive individuals who feed on the blood of the widows, who grow rich out of the substances of the ward they administer. There are vindictive individuals who carry out terrible actions of revenge, yet they look like peaceful and beneficent people. Let them alone, let them alone. The day of the Lord will come. He will uncover all the iniquities of earth.

After they sinned, God offered Adam and Eve a skin of an animal to clothe themselves with. On the day of judgment by the Lord, however, no cover whatsoever will be offered. Hypocrites will appear before everyone in all the deformity that belongs to wicked sinners. Do you think that they will regret being so wickedly advised? There will be no more time for that.

4. Do you know what is set for them, the swindlers, the hypocrites, the wicked? Go over a page of Holy Scripture. The rich man who banqueted along with friends and dignitaries, the one who, like a watching prince was considered worthy of all honors, in a moment passed away and immediately tumbled down into hell. Then the wretched poor Lazarus died, the one who pitifully longed for the

crumbs that fell from the table of the rich man. Now Lazarus was taken to heaven to be in the bosom of the holy Abraham.

This is, at last, the fortune that belongs to patient Christians. They have paradise as their recompense. Instead the evil ones have the fire of hell as their eternal punishment. Therefore, should the prosperity of the evil ones be ever envied?... They enjoy themselves, yes, but they do like the oxen that feed and get fat at the manger, set to be slaughtered on the following day.

5. Do we want to find out what will happen to us one day? Let us see how we are in these days at the time of tribulation. In the fervor of our prayer we promise to the Lord to remain faithful to him up to Mt. Calvary, as Peter the Apostle did. Yet who can assure us that our resolutions will be effective or not? What really proves it is the tribulation that the Lord sends to us. At that moment if we will be submissive to it, it will be a sign for us of eternal predestination. Yet, they who complain and curse and manifestly turn against God to accuse his Providence, these must certainly have reason to fear, since they are not able to stand the trial that God offers to them.

How much should we ourselves fear! And how heartily should we embrace the trials of tribulation that God sends on our way! It is so important that we welcome with great resignation those trials, as we care for being awarded the kingdom in paradise.

6. Behold the judgment of the Lord! It is given by means of fire. Through fire at the end of the world the earth will be purified. That fire will illumine the elect so that they will come forth glorious. Fire will not hurt them at all, but will brighten them. On the contrary, fire will torment the

reprobates with utmost ardor. At the particular judgment the fire of purgatory tests the elect who are not clean enough yet to be ready to enter heaven. In the midst of that fire the souls of the just love God and along with the torment they also experience consolation. The fire waiting for the reprobates is the fire of hell, which is a furious and desperate blaze. The day of tribulation has its own fire, too, which consists of weariness and torment which, like fire, come with the wicked tribulations of the flesh, avarice and pride, or even the physical pains of the body or the impressions left on the heart by the unjust vexations of the evil.

St. Paul says that he experienced so many of such tribulations in Asia that he could not overcome them by nature. Yet God always added his grace. Grace acted in such a way that at the time of tribulation St. Paul experienced most vivid consolations. Likewise, the wicked have their own tribulations, but they do not receive any consolation from above, no support in themselves, and consequently they only experience the torment of that fire. What do you think about that, my brothers and sisters?... Do you think that we should fear the judgment of the Lord?... Yes, indeed! And very much so! Let us fear the judgments that result in condemnation. Let us have confidence in the judgments that acquit.

REFLECTIONS

1. Remove the mask!
2. God puts aside for himself three days to deliver a judgment.
3. In the days of the judgment of the Lord true virtue will be seen as well as the hidden vice of men.

4. Hell is set for the wicked, paradise for the just ones of the Lord.
5. One day we will be what we are in the moment of tribulation.
6. Let us pick now the judgment that we will like to have one day.

GOSPEL OF THE TWENTY-THIRD SUNDAY AFTER PENTECOST

One more remedy not to die

1. Dying is the act that frightens greatly most of the people. Fools, however, are those who die! No one dies unless he wants to die out of his own will. Because death comes only through mortal sin. He who shuns away mortal sin, does not die in his soul. Nor does he die in his body, because, though it has been said that even the just man must descend into his grave, it is also true that he remains there only temporarily, as if sleeping in his bed. It is true that from there his body will then move into the life of paradise.

What is important above all is the remedy, if there is one, not to sin. The good God gave it to us. The Lord says in the book of *Sirach*: "In whatever you do, remember your last days, and you will never sin."[1] The divine Savior at the bedside of the ill or by the bier of the dead worked his miracles of mercy. Listen to what today's Gospel says.

"Before Jesus had finished speaking to the disciples of John, a synagogue leader came up, did him reverence, and said: 'My daughter has just died. Please come and lay your hand on her and she will come back to life.' Jesus stood up and followed him, and his disciples did the same. As they were going, a woman who had suffered from hemorrhages for twelve years came up behind him and touched the tassel on his cloak. 'If only I can touch his cloak,' she thought, 'I will get well.' Jesus turned around and saw her and said,

---

[1] Sir 7:36

246

'Courage, daughter! Your faith has restored you to health.' That very moment the woman got well. When Jesus arrived at the synagogue leader's house and saw the flute players and the crowd who were making a din, he said, 'Leave, all of you! The little girl is not dead. She is alseep.' At this they began to ridicule him. When the crowd had been put out he entered and took her by the hand, and the little girl got up. News of this circulated throughout the district."[1]

How beneficially the presence of death helps to wake up the spirits, to lead them on the path of good! Let us think of it a little. We will find out how true is the saying of the Lord: "He who remembers the last things will never sin."

2. Not to sin anymore is the desire of the just souls. St. Teresa longed for dying so that she could be out of danger of sinning any more. St. Aloysius Gonzaga macerated his body with so many penances so that he could remove ever more from himself the danger of sin. Do we want not to sin any more? Let us keep present in our mind death and the terrible truths that follow it, that is the judgment of Jesus Christ, paradise and hell.

St. Methodius, the apostle of Bulgary, not knowing what other means to resort to to convert the pagan king of that country, had recourse to painting on a very large canvas the scenes of death, the judgment, hell and paradise. Then he showed it to the king and asked him to look at it for sometime every day. That was enough. The king soon began to ask: "I want to be baptized a Christian, because I want my eternal salvation."

If this truth makes an errant man repent and give life to a dead pagan, what will it not do to the mind and heart of a

---

[1] Mt 9:18-26

faithful Christian? It preserves him from sinning. It is a matter of faith.: he who remembers the last things will never sin." What is helpful in this case? Are you expected to think of death in all the hours and every minute? Meditate on death every day for a little while, for this is necessary. During the rest of the day it will be enough to think of it here and there. Isn't the Lord reasonable in that?... So, if you pay attention to this, you will be saved.

3. Yet, see to it that this thought of death is not just a superficial remembrance of it. It must be a reflection on it that reaches the recesses of your mind, that moves the affections of your heart. To this end, you need to think not only of death, but also of the judgment of the Lord that takes place right after, and of the sentence causing acquittal or condemnation, paradise or hell.

He who does not think of these according to holy faith, cannot count on much good. There are many who remember that they have to die, yet what do they get out of it? They do as those mentioned in the *Book of Wisdom* are found to say: "We have to die; once we are dead, everything is over. So, then, let us enjoy ourselves as much as we can."[1] Drinking and eating happily for the few days of life is what the fools look for. Very foolish, indeed they are, for they do not remember or do not want to make provisions for the still terrible judgments which God has set for us. Let us fear death and let us fear even more the outcome of the judgment to come as well as of the eternity, happy or unhappy, that will follow.

---

[1] See Wis 2:3-6

4. The Lord says: "Remember the last things and you will never sin." Do you know of a reason that will convince you of this more easily? Meditate on it. To walk straight here on earth prudence is needed to act uprightly, and this is inspired by the thought of death. He who thinks that he may die at any moment, do you suppose he will be willing to do anything disorderly?

Furthermore, to live holily one needs justice. To justice's support comes the judgment, particular or general. He who thinks that he will give account to the Lord of every word he says and every thought he has, is it possible that he will not guard himself against offending anyone in any way?...

Then, we need temperance, and to this purpose it is very helpful to think of hell! He who indulges in the sinful pleasures of the flesh will have the fires of hell as his punishment. Now, who is going to be so crazy as to be ready to give in to the sinful pleasures of the senses and then burn in hell for eternity?

Finally, to walk uprightly one needs fortitude, which is supplied by the thought of paradise. Looking forward to that blessedness, fearless Christians exclaim: "The good I am looking for is so great that every pain is a pleasure for me." With this great thought in their mind, they strengthen the cardinal virtues, which are the foundation of religious life.

5. Going back over again to what I said before, that it is not enough to think of death in abstract in order not to sin, but one must think of it concretely, namely that death will affect him, that it might happen at any time, and so on and so forth.

St. Jerome, a holy doctor, at prayer or asleep, always kept a skull at his side to talk to or sleep on, safely. St.

Francis Borgia, thinking of death, and more precisely meditating on it, became so involved with death as if he were already dead, even laying motionless and lost in his senses. Do we think of death in this way?... Yet, if we still commit many sins, it means that we are not able to take much advantage of the thought of death as a remedy against the death of sin.

6. Many can be found who do not think of death and judgment to come, because they are scared by it. However, how can they be scared, when Scripture teaches and the wise experience that the thought of the last things removes all feelings of gloom? Gloom is the result of seeing darkness. On the contrary, he who properly thinks of death and directs his life holily towards it, immediately finds serenity in his spirit. With death the danger of offending God over and over again by sin ends. With death also all the afflictions of the spirit as well as the ailments of the body end. Death is the merciful mother who entrusts us to Jesus' arms. And who does not know that Jesus, our savior, is a merciful father! Pointing at paradise he says to us: "Let us ascend on high, for it is right that the house of the Father be for ever the dwelling for the son who always has believed and trusted in the Father's bounty." In so saying, we will go up on high with Jesus Christ.

I beg you, then, don't you ever say that death saddens one's spirit. Death consoles it and comforts it a lot. It removes sin from one's heart, and along with it all the calamities that are connected with iniquity. It is very true, indeed, that the thought of the last things is a remedy against sin, and consequently against death. Let us think of them and may our soul live forever.

REFLECTIONS

1. A remedy for not dying.
2. He who thinks of the last things never sins.
3. One needs to think of death along with the judgment, hell and paradise.
4. This thought grows strong in attaining the cardinal virtues.
5. The remembrance of the last things must penetrate the recesses of our heart.
6. The thought of the last things comforts one's spirit, and does not distress it.

GOSPEL OF THE TWENTY-FOURTH SUNDAY AFTER PENTECOST

At the end of everything of this world

1. Men, men, what do we do here on earth? We spend so many energies for the things here below and talk so much for the enjoyment of this world. Yet at the end of it what is awaiting us? Death awaits us, and right after it the judgment of the Lord. What a terrible expectation! Listen, now, to the entire discourse of the Gospel that concerns this, and let us be horrified in the depths of our hearts.

Jesus said to his disciples: "When you see the abominable and destructive thing which the prophet Daniel foretold standing on holy ground (let the reader take note!), those in Judea must flee to the mountains. If a man is on the roof terrace, he must not come down to get anything out of his house. If a man is in the field, he must not turn back to pick up his cloak. It will be hard on pregnant women or nursing mothers in those days. Keep praying that you will not have to flee in winter or on a sabbath, for those days will be more filled with anguish than any from the beginning of the world until now or in all ages to come. Indeed, if the period had not been shortened, not a human being would be saved. For the sake of the chosen, however, the days will be shortened.

If anyone tells you at that time, 'Look, the Messiah is here,' or 'He is there,' do not believe it. False messiahs and false prophets will appear, performing signs and wonders so great as to mislead even the chosen if that were possible. Remember, I have told you all about it beforehand; so if they tell you, 'Look, He is in the desert,' do not go out there; or 'He is in innermost rooms,' do not believe it. As the lightning from the east flashes to the west, so will the coming of the Son of Man be. Where the carcass lies, there the vultures gather. Immediately after the stress of that period, 'the sun will be darkened, the moon will not shed her light, the stars will fall from the sky, and the hosts of heaven will be shaken loose.' Then the sign of the Son of Man will appear in the sky, and 'all the clans of earth will strike their breasts' as they see 'the Son of Man coming on the clouds of heaven' with power and great glory. He will dispatch his angels 'with a mighty trumpet blast, and they will assemble his chosen from the four winds, from one end of the heavens to the other.'

From the fig tree learn a lesson. When its branch grows tender and sprouts leaves, you realize that summer is near. Likewise, when you see these things happening, you will know that he is near, standing at your door. I assure you, the present generation will not pass away until all this takes place. The heavens and the earth will pass away but my words will not pass."[1]

This is, then, our end, my brothers and sisters: to fall under the judgment of the Lord. At the final judgment we will all be judged in front of the universe. At the particular judgment each one will be judged separately. St. Paul reminds the Hebrews: "It is appointed that men die once, and after death be judged."[2] Let us fear much more, because death and the judgment of the Lord alike might surprise us anytime.

2. It has been established by divine law that we must die. We must die because we are sinners. Unfortunate Adam

---

[1] Mt 24: 15-35
[2] Heb 9:27

when he sinned! In placing him in the midst of the Garden of Eden, the Lord set Adam to be the king of the universe and said to him: "You will not die on condition that you obey me by never touching the fruits of that tree." If they had obeyed, Adam and Eve would have been always agile, always happy, always full of life, and would have lived for many centuries, until God would have taken them from earth into heaven. Unfortunately the miserable ones wanted to rebel and therefore they immediately found out what that command meant: "You will die!" Now you see why sin is regarded by everyone as the utmost evil here below.

All of us, then, will die, even though those who will die last and will be closer to the final judgment will remain in the grave for a shorter time. Those who will live up to the final moment must die first to rise again immediately, when shortly after the angel will sound his trumpet. This will happen at the end of everything. Let us not bother much with the things of earth, for after all we all have to die.

3. Adam and Eve died even though they were shaped out of clay with so much care by the very hands of God. Lamech, Mahalalel and Methuselah died, who seemed to defy death by living one seven hundred years, the other eight hundred, and the third over nine hundred years. The patriarchs and the prophets died. The apostles of the divine Savior died, the pure virgins, and the unconquered confessors as well. In our days most illustrious personages have died who seemed not to have to die for the sake of souls. Then, we, too, will die. Didn't Jesus Christ, who is the Holy of Holies, die? Didn't the Virgin Mary, who is the true mother of the Savior, pure and immaculate, die? We, who are miserable sinners, will certainly die. yet, if we have to die,

why do we attach our hearts so much to the things of this earth?

4. Worse still, since we can only die once. Once the soul has left the body, there is no hope that it will join it again. After our remains have been taken to the cemetery, there is no way that we will come to life and take over again our house and fields we had left behind. Very true, Jesus Christ raised Lazarus and after some time he let him die again. Yet this is a miracle of such rare occurrence that we would be too presumptious or simpleminded to believe that God would show such a great favor on our behalf.

Once we are dead, we do not return to this earth. So, if we are not going to come back here, why don't we see to it that we set out holily for the journey that will be our last one? We have only one chance to die, so let us see to it that we die in the arms of no one else other than the Lord's.

5. The Lord is the one who is going to judge us. We will expire in the place and after the illness that only God knows. If there will be anyone assisting us at that time, he will check if our heart will be still beating, or our breath still coming out of our mouth. Yet we will be dead by then. At that very instant our life career is over. At that very moment the Lord will appear to judge us. The soul will give her last look at the body, a corpse, and will present herself at the tribunal of God. She will be there alone. She will carry along the bundle of the good and evil she had done. Other than that, she will be alone, alone awaiting for the sentence.

The poor soul will not even be able to speak to justify herself, because God knows everything. She will not even be able to ask for mercy, because now it is the time for justice. In case she is in grave fear, she will not even be able to flee, because the Lord is the omnipotent. The poor soul will have the ones to accuse her: her conscience, her guardian angel, the holy law of the Lord which she violated. Her accusers will also be the senseless creatures like the sun and the earth that witnessed her actions.

What will we be doing there in the meantime?... If we do not know what to do or what to think of, the Lord will see to it. In a moment he weighs, counts and divides. In a moment he comes up with the sentence. Great God! In a moment we die. In a moment we find ourselves before God and in front of the abyss of eternity. In a moment the Lord awards us with paradise or hell, and we barely think with some kind of fear that right after death there is the judgment of the Lord!

6. Nor will that judgment be the only one. Because, in a matter of time, there will be one more. Isn't it true that many have gone through here who were believed to be good and instead were found guilty, while others who were believed to be bad were found to be good? Isn't it true also that everyone, good or bad, live on after death in the reputation of everyone? A father, who has edified his children to do good or has scandalized them by his evildoing, will inspire them for many generations to imitate him in doing good things or wrong things.

Besides, he who will leave behind examples of good or evil, or he who above all will leave behind good or evil writings, will leave a source that for a long time will generate good or evil. How many souls are still being saved because of the writings of St. John Chrysostom? By the same token, how many souls will be taken to perdition down the centuries because of the writings of Martin Luther?

At last the final judgment will take place at the end of the world. That will be a most terrible one. The day on which it will take place is referred to as the "great day", a day of great grief. The Gospel's passage that we have read horrifies us. Still, the fear stirred in us by the Gospel's page is nothing but the preparation or foreword for the last day. What will it be like when finally God comes to judge? What will it be?... "Woe," cries out in horror St. Augustine, "woe to the Christian who, in order to believe in these things wants to experience them."

REFLECTIONS

1. At the end of everything there will be death and then the judgment.
2. Sin is the cause of death.
3. Actually, everyone dies.
4. Everyone dies only once.
5. After death, there is the particular or individual judgment of the Lord.
6. At the final judgment, which will take place at the end of the world, God will judge altogether, all human beings, in the universality of whatever was caused by them up to that day.

WRITINGS OF
BLESSED LOUIS GUANELLA
in English

1. Anthology of all his writings
2. Regulations of the Servants of Charity - 1910
3. Norms for the Houses of the Servants of Charity
4. Circular letters to the Servants of Charity
5. Let us go to the Father
6. Let us go to the mountain of happiness
7. The Foundation
8. In the sacred time
9. Remembrances of St. Teresa of Avila
10. The little poor man of Christ
11. The Third Order of St. Francis and the
        Encyclical Letter of Leo XIII
12. The mountaineer
13. One hundred praises... of B. Andrew of Peschiera
14. The ways of Divine Providence
15. Outlines
16. In the month of fervor
17. In the month of flowers
18. A salute to the Immaculate Mary of Lourdes
19. The bread of the soul (Three Volumes)
20. Spirituality for the Guanellian Family
21. The little way

Type-setting: pdt
East Providence, RI
Printed at Havertown Printing Co - Broomall, PA
1999